Mission Statement

Redeeming love has been my theme, and shall be 'til I die.
THERE IS A FOUNTAIN FILLED WITH BLOOD by William Cowper

There is nothing like the funeral service of a follower of Christ, one who confessed their hope and faith in Jesus Christ and lived accordingly. In fact, most of these services are celebrations or "homegoings"—we know the deceased is already present with God and enjoying their eternal reward.

Instead of desolation and hopelessness, there is quiet assurance. Instead of doubt, there is peace. Instead of mourning what could have been, friends and loved ones take comfort in knowing that God set the boundaries—every day of this person's life was ordained by Him. We who remain get the joy of remembering how Jesus shone through them.

What makes the difference—in life and in death? Redeeming love. It's as simple as that. Redeeming love transforms our lives and recasts the meaning of our deaths.

Do the people who know you understand that God has redeemed your life? Do they recognize that you're different because of Him? If not, what needs to change? After all, our days on earth are numbered. Let's make them count.

Read Psalm 36:9
Lord, thank You for redeeming me—let every aspect of my life shout that truth.

Divine Dialogue

Tempted and tried, I need a great Savior, One who can help my burdens to bear.
I Must Tell Jesus by Elisha A. Hoffman

Who do you call first when there's news to share or a problem to solve? A spouse, parent, sibling, or friend? Whether the news is good or bad, do you ever first think to share the experience or emotion with Jesus? Sure, He already knows the details, but it is in the act of sharing that our spirit is blessed or our burden lightened.

What we share with Jesus in confidence, prayer, or thanksgiving is never misunderstood or ignored. He then strengthens us by His Word and reveals Himself in our situation.

Having lived as a man, Jesus understands our trials and temptations; He has experienced the attacks of our enemy and is uniquely able to be both Savior and supportive friend.

So while people around us may lend a willing ear, let's first go tell Jesus and seek guidance from Him who is able to affect both our hearts and circumstances.

Read Proverbs 2:6
Lord, talking with You doubles my joy and halves my sorrow.

Faith Builders

For if I'd never had a problem, I wouldn't know that He could solve them,
I'd never know what faith in God could do.

THROUGH IT ALL by Andrae Crouch

After more than ten years of trying to conceive a baby, Jack and Tammy ___ to adopt a child. Within a year they were thrilled to connect with a young woman who thought they would be ideal parents. But the baby boy was born prematurely and weighed less than two pounds. It didn't matter to Jack and Tammy. The couple adored their son, and for weeks they joyously watched him grow and flourish. Tragically, their little boy died of complications when he was four months old. How did the couple cope?

their grief, Jack and Tammy took time to give God the glory for their son's life. They openly praised the Lord for the gift of life and love, and they held on to their faith. They allowed God to use their greatest heartache to show where they drew their comfort from.

Could you do the same?

Read Psalm 13:5
Lord, keep me trusting in You, through it all!

The Sweetest Hour

And since He bids me seek His face, believe His Word and trust His grace,
I'll cast on Him my ev'ry care.

SWEET HOUR OF PRAYER by William W. Walford

A personal invitation to a special event makes you feel uniquely wanted. The thought that our awesome God allows us to come into His presence through prayer is incredible; but the fact that He offers—even requests it—is downright miraculous.

In Proverbs 3 Solomon admonishes us to trust in the Lord and not depend on our own knowledge but allow Him to direct us. In His mercy, our powerful God can shoulder our burdens—we can rely on Him to bring about what is best for us in His timing. And it's marvelous to consider that the Creator of the universe graciously waits for us to commit our concerns to Him. He's invited us to do so.

Do you have a private time and place designated for just you and God to spend time together? Time spent in personal fellowship with your heavenly Father will be returned to you in ways you never imagined.

Read Acts 3:1
I come to You and lay all my petitions on Your altar, God.

Face Time

In the secret, in the quiet place, in the stillness you are there.
IN THE SECRET by Andy Park

Working, parenting, friending, serving, cleaning, shopping, exercising, driving, and, occasionally, after that long list, sleeping. We each have our list of "ings"—those activities that keep us so busy that we rarely find time for intimacy with another person, let alone time with the Savior. Yet Jesus encourages His disciples to go into their secret closet and pray to their Father in heaven (Matthew 6:6).

He desires to hear from His followers on earth. He wants an ongoing acknowledgment of His holy presence, even if He is unseen. A genuine relationship with Him requires ongoing communication; no matter where we are or what we are doing, our God wants us to be mindful of His presence. And while we carry Him throughout our day, He invites us to also dedicate time to push away from the noise and seek His face without distraction.

Read 1 Kings 19:11–13
Dear Father, help me seek undistracted communion with You each day.

January 9

Today's Challenge, Tomorrow's Blessing

Every blessing You pour out I'll turn back to praise.
BLESSED BE YOUR NAME by Matt and Beth Redman

As the US housing market began to decline in the midst of a struggling economy, a young family—in response to a new job opportunity—relocated to a completely new part of the country, leaving behind an unsold house.

Month after month passed, and the empty house remained on the market. For more than a year the family struggled, paying two mortgages and sometimes questioning the purpose behind the financial burden. What was the point?

Today, however, their perspective has changed. They often share how God sustained their family—providing adequate income, preserving their credit, and, ultimately, sending a buyer at the most critical point. When they thought giving up might be the best option, Jesus drew them into complete reliance on Him. Nowadays, they consider themselves most blessed.

Read Acts 2:17–18
God, thank You for the abundance of blessings that come from You.

Follow the Leader

That You would guide me in every single step I take.
EVERYDAY by Joel Houston

What did David, Gideon, Joshua, and Caleb have in common? They all sought the Lord for direction before they took action—and the Lord answered them. Certainly we still seek Him today, but things are a little different for us. Too often we don't recognize His voice because we're expecting burning bushes, voices from heaven, and parting seas. But God has more ways of getting through to us than we give Him credit for.

So, how do we hear God's voice today? Does He still speak? The answer is a resounding yes. Sometimes we need to be still to hear Him over life's commotion. Other times, His will is made plain through a series of events—one door after another opening as we take the next step.

Regardless of how He accomplishes it, Jesus promised He would reveal Himself to us through His Word and by the power of the Holy Spirit. Because He does so, we must watch, and wait, and follow Him in faith.

Read Psalm 119:105
Lord, I look to You to lead me in the paths of righteousness.

Perpetual Praise

To the going down of the same, the Lord's name is to be praised.
FROM THE RISING OF THE SUN by Paul. S. Deming

As the morning dawns, you have coffee or juice in hand and are ready to accomplish big things, giving God thanks for new opportunities to "get it right." By noon, you've encountered some challenging situations but are still gratefully forging ahead. By dinner, you're frustrated and questioning what the point of the day was.

Can you relate? God hasn't changed; only your circumstances did. But that's enough to throw us off sometimes, to make our attitude "adjust" in the wrong direction.

Here's the good news: whatever is going on around us doesn't have to determine when, or if, God is worthy to be praised. He is always worthy of our worship. He deserves our honor from sunup to sundown.

How do you characterize God and His goodness? Look beyond your circumstances and look to your mighty God—and praise Him.

Read Psalm 113:3
Gracious God, I will praise You for who You are, regardless of what I face today.

Engulfed

Underneath me, all around me, is the current of Thy love—
leading onward, leading homeward, to Thy glorious rest above.
O THE DEEP, DEEP LOVE OF JESUS by Samuel Trevor Francis

An ocean current is a continuous, directed movement of water. It's powered by forces like wind, temperature, gravitational pull, and the contours of the ocean floor. However, surface currents make up only 10 percent of all the water in the ocean; the movement of deep water is driven by its density and temperature. The power and energy of the water—either up top or down deep—is intense and has a dramatic effect on things in its path.

Like the ocean current, Christ's powerful love can be a constant and moving force in our lives. Through the conviction and influence of the Holy Spirit, He envelops us. As our relationship deepens and we allow Christ to lead us, He will use the influences and events of our lives to continually compel us to a closer walk with Him, guiding our steps to an eternity with Him.

Read Romans 8:37–39
Christ, Your love completely surrounds me.
What would I do without that protection?

Unparalleled

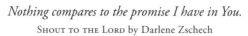

Nothing compares to the promise I have in You.
SHOUT TO THE LORD by Darlene Zschech

Comparison shopping is a part of our culture. Whether it's price and quality or reputation and durability, we like to be assured we've made a good selection. So we evaluate our options by doing side-by-side assessments—comparing "apples to apples."

Such a judgment is far more difficult to conduct when it comes to the Object of our faith. After all, try to compare your options: salvation through Jesus and...?

That's just it! We are blessed to be able to rest on the promises of God. Nothing else man may offer can match the peace and security found in our heavenly Father. No other faith gives us such open access to the Creator. He loved us before we knew Him, provided our sin sacrifice when we were still lost, and graciously forgave us before we were willing to admit that we needed it. There is no other god before Him.

Read 1 Chronicles 16:23–27
O Lord, You are holy, mighty, and magnificent— the one true God!

Reconciled to the Father

No other way to be reconciled, to receive complete forgiveness.
I See the Cross by Brian Doerksen

Marriage counselors and family therapists often talk of the importance of reconciliation between family members. It's a critical step because so often hostility can grow to a point where each party has been profoundly hurt or betrayed.

Reconciliation means that the parties reunite, all former hostility is removed, and peaceful and loving kinship and communication are restored. The Bible teaches of man's reconciliation with his Creator.

When Adam and Eve sinned in the garden, humankind was estranged from God. Their sin offended God and created a chasm between the Creator and His creation. This breach could only be bridged by the suffering, death, and resurrection of Jesus Christ. The blood of Jesus not only erased the sin that separated us from God, it brought us back into peace and communion with Him.

Read Isaiah 59:2–3
Jesus, thank You for reconciling us with You.

Busy Work

I need Thy presence every passing hour.

ABIDE WITH ME by Henry F. Lyte

Does it ever feel like the busier you become, the less time you spend seeking God? Sure, you go to church every Sunday and even regularly attend midweek Bible study, but how much time do you take to seek Him in your personal time—on your own?

Day after day we rush through our hectic schedules and forget that taking time to abide in God is an essential part of our faith walk. There's no doubt that in no time at all, life can get very busy. But spending time with God each day is the best way to draw nearer to Him.

Jesus promises, "I will never leave you nor forsake you" (Hebrews 13:5 NKJV). Isn't it a relief to know that even though we sometimes get too busy for God, He's never too busy for us? Make time to daily abide in the presence of the Almighty; it will give new meaning, depth, and perspective to every day.

Read 1 John 2:28

Lord, forgive me if I have allowed my busy schedule to take precedence over spending time in Your presence.

First Love

You are the living Truth! All wisdom dwells in You, the Source of every skill, the One eternal.
We Come, O Christ, to You by Margaret Clarkson

Think back to your first love—the first person you gave your heart to; that person you thought you would never be able to live without. Did you spend countless hours in conversation hanging on their every word, trying to learn every detail about them?

God wants you to come to Him in a similar way each and every day to learn about His heart and mind. He invites you to sit in His presence, for that's where you'll discover how to use your skills and abilities for His glory. He wants you to learn new things about Him so you two can be even closer.

How incredible it is that we have access to His wisdom, His power, His purposes! Take the time to get to know who He is. His understanding and grace can be your foundation, and His constant love can become the source of your joy.

Read John 6:68

Heavenly Father, thank You for pursuing me. Help me to return Your passion.

Closer than a Brother

Hallelujah! What a Savior! Hallelujah! What a friend!
Saving, helping, keeping, loving, He is with me to the end.
Jesus! What a Friend for Sinners by J. Wilbur Chapman

As children we don't often truly appreciate our siblings. Instead we spend time battling over toys, privileges, and attention. On the flip side, as parents we find ourselves trying to persuade our kids that their brother or sister is going to be an advocate, friend, and confidant throughout life. They are the ones who will walk together through the ups and downs of life.

Even more so is this principle true with our Lord and Savior, Jesus Christ, who has made a way for us to experience an abundant life both now and for eternity. He is the friend who sticks closer than a brother—no matter what life may throw our way, Jesus is there as our most intimate friend and support.

Seek to know Jesus—read His Word; talk to Him in prayer. He is there, loving and caring for you all the way until you meet Him face-to-face.

Read Romans 8:35–39
Gracious Lord, thank You for being a friend that sticks closer than a brother.

Universal Wealth

When we reach the end of our hoarded resources, our Father's full giving is only begun.
He Giveth More Grace by Annie Johnson Flint

According to the US Census, the average household income in 2009 was just over $52,000—second only to Switzerland's, which was $54,000. Compare that to the average income of an individual in Africa: $365 a year, or $1 per day. It's incredible to think of the gap that exists, isn't it? But regardless of where we live or our economic condition, we all have one thing in common: our need for a Savior.

For those of us in first-world countries, we have an abundance of "stuff." From the more permanent—such as property—to the disposable like food or entertainment, we are blessed to have our physical needs met as well as obtaining many of our "wants." Our wealth is only the tip of the iceberg of God's goodness to us. In His great grace, He has made all humans richer than we could imagine by providing victory over sin and the grave.

Read 2 Corinthians 9:8
You are good, God. All the time.

Generous Grace

But the wonder of wonders that thrills my soul is the wonder that God loves me.
THE WONDER OF IT ALL by George Beverly Shea

Have you thought about it lately—the fact that the Creator of the universe loves you? The Author of eternity, who "was" even before time began, is personally engaged in your life and has redeemed you for His purposes.

In chapter 8 of Paul's letter to the Romans, he declares that he is convinced that nothing on earth and no distance can separate us from the love of God. Our relationship with God is a miracle. How else do you explain such a perfect, holy love—with no boundaries, no conditions, no strings—extending itself to such sinful creatures as we are?

Because of Jesus, we are more than blessed; we are more than conquerors over sin—we have found favor with God! Let that sink in to your heart and mind. Through Jesus, God is whispering to you now, "I love you."

Read John 15:12
I praise You, God, for Your unconditional love!

One Way

Every day a brand new chance to say, Jesus, You are the only way.
My Savior Lives by Jon Egan and Glenn Packiam

GPS devices direct us to destinations near and far. They are wonderful inventions—guiding us through uncertain turns and along unknown roads...until we find ourselves in new construction zones that have not yet been uploaded to the system. When that happens, we're left wondering which way to go.

In familiar territory, we often recover quickly. Even without the GPS, we might know an alternate route. If it's an unknown locale, however, finding our way can be more troublesome. We may end up on the right road, but not without some anxiety.

Thankfully, though events of each day are unknown, the wisdom of God guides us peacefully through both familiar and uncharted territory. It illuminates our path, helping us to clearly see opportunities and obstacles. It teaches us how to set boundary lines that enable us to follow God's will.

There is only one way for the Christian: God's way. Ask Him to keep you on course, now and always.

Read John 14:6
I know Your way is the only way, Lord. Help me stay on track.

Released and Rejoicing

And when from death I'm free, I'll sing and joyful be, and thro' eternity I'll sing on.
WHAT WONDROUS LOVE IS THIS, American folk song, attributed to Alexander Means

Seventeen years after his wrongful incarceration, North Carolina native Greg Taylor was pardoned from a life sentence in prison. Life for him was suddenly, radically different—and he wasn't about to forget it. Since that liberating day, Mr. Taylor has been actively spreading the word about how to avoid his fate. He makes the most of his independence and this second chance to truly live.

In much the same way, we believers have been acquitted and released from the burden of sin's hold on our lives. We were doomed to a punishing eternity, separate from God. Yet when we placed our faith in Jesus and His saving work, we were set free. We have our own good news—the best—to celebrate and share with our neighbors.

Don't hesitate to spread the word to others in your community. After all, they need pardon too.

Read Deuteronomy 21:23
I praise You for providing me a pardon from all my sins.

Paid in Full

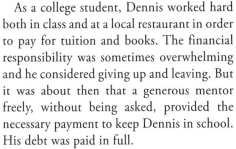

And when before the throne I stand in Him complete,
"Jesus died my soul to save," my lips shall still repeat.
JESUS PAID IT ALL by Elvina M. Hall

As a college student, Dennis worked hard both in class and at a local restaurant in order to pay for tuition and books. The financial responsibility was sometimes overwhelming and he considered giving up and leaving. But it was about then that a generous mentor freely, without being asked, provided the necessary payment to keep Dennis in school. His debt was paid in full.

What would be your response if you were in Dennis's shoes? What if Dennis had a chance to sit down with the donor and thank him?

You have the opportunity today to do just that with the One who relieved you of your debt to sin. Jesus gave of Himself to save your soul when you most needed it—when you were in the depths of sin. He did it just for you. Take a few moments to sit down with Him and tell Him what His sacrifice has meant to you personally. There's no freedom like the freedom He has provided!

Read 1 Corinthians 7:23
Thank You, Jesus, for saving my soul.

Blood Purchase

He is our Rock, our hope of eternal salvation; hail Him, hail Him, Jesus the crucified!
Praise Him! Praise Him! by Fanny J. Crosby

With Christ as our personal Savior, giving thanks is a throughout-the-day worship opportunity. Our greatest reason to give Him thanks, of course, is for sacrificing Himself to save us. Praising His name for this alone never becomes tiresome or repetitious in God's ears.

In Revelation 5, John reassures, "Do not weep! See, the Lion of the tribe of Judah, the Root of David, has triumphed" (verse 5 NIV). Jesus triumphed over sin and death. Eternal salvation was purchased when He willingly shed His redeeming blood through crucifixion. Every tribe, language, people, and nation in this entire world is covered by Christ's sacrifice, if they will accept His precious gift of life.

This is why we hope, why we rejoice, why we praise Him! Worthy is the Lamb that was slain!

Read Revelation 5:9
My hope, Lord Jesus, is in You. You are my Rock, my Deliverer.

Trusted Source

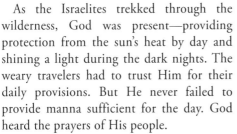

Thus deriving from their banner light by night and shade by day,
safe they feed upon the manna, which He gives them when they pray.
GLORIOUS THINGS OF THEE ARE SPOKEN by John Newton

As the Israelites trekked through the wilderness, God was present—providing protection from the sun's heat by day and shining a light during the dark nights. The weary travelers had to trust Him for their daily provisions. But He never failed to provide manna sufficient for the day. God heard the prayers of His people.

Similarly, God is a constant source of strength and provision in our lives. With overflowing love and kindness, God is the foundation of our life. He knows our needs before we even ask Him; He graciously and faithfully supplies them today so we can have hope for tomorrow.

What prayer have you spoken to God today? Perhaps you're grieving a loss, stressed out over finances, or concerned about a health problem. You can trust God with your concerns. Share your needs with Him and He will provide you with manna for today.

Read Psalm 87:3
You hear my prayers. Thank You.

Crowning Day

Crown Him the Lord of life who triumphed o'er the grave,
who rose victorious in the strife for those He came to save.
CROWN HIM WITH MANY CROWNS by Matthew Bridges and Godfrey Thring

The weather on June 2, 1953, was dismal in England. It poured rain. Nevertheless, the streets of London were filled with people waiting to see the procession of the newly crowned Queen Elizabeth II. Thousands of brand-new television sets came to life as people tuned in to watch the queen's coronation. Ultimately, millions of people viewed the crowning ceremony.

As Jesus traveled through the crowded streets of Jerusalem, He wore no gold or jewels atop His head. His crown was one of thorns. People did not cheer Him, they jeered Him. He journeyed not to His coronation but to His death.

Yet Jesus ultimately triumphed over the grave. He regained His rightful throne three days later, as the risen King, the Prince of Peace. And He left us, a royal priesthood of believers, to carry on the work of His kingdom.

Read Revelation 19:12
Dear Lord, what a gift You give us in providing new life through You!

Pardoned

With His blood He purchased me. On the Cross He sealed my pardon,
paid the debt and made me free.

I Will Sing of My Redeemer by Philip P. Bliss

After her twenty-five-year sentence was commuted to time served, a young woman sentenced for a minor, nonviolent offense was set free. After her release, the woman honored those in prison—who also deserve relief—by fasting for justice. Since then, the woman has attended law school and started her own foundation to help those incarcerated.

The blood of Jesus offers everyone freedom from sin—it cleanses, purifies, and pays the debt so we are free to commune with God.

We can rejoice. Jesus's sacrifice on the cross paid the debt that we could not satisfy. Thank God, we are free. We have a new life through Christ because we have been forgiven.

You are free to worship because Jesus redeemed you. As Savior, the precious Lamb of God paid the price for your sins. How will you honor Him today?

Read Job 19:25

Jesus, you set me free! Help me never to forget Your redeeming ways.

Transformed

How marvelous! How wonderful! And my song shall ever be:
How marvelous! How wonderful! Is my Savior's love for me!
I STAND AMAZED by Charles H. Gabriel

There are seven natural wonders of the world: the Grand Canyon, Victoria Falls, the Great Barrier Reef, Mount Everest, Aurora, the Harbor of Rio de Janeiro, and Paricutin volcano. People travel thousands of miles to gaze at these amazing views. Their grandeur renders us speechless.

To believers, these incredible formations testify of the magnificence of our Creator. But He has performed a similar magnificent work inside each of us. God has taken our sin-sick souls, our messed-up lives, and transformed them. He has carved out vast valleys of heartache and sent His river of life flowing through them. He has revitalized desolate deserts of the soul, planting lush gardens inside us that continue to grow. And who is tending it all as the Master Gardener of our soul? The Holy Spirit, who leads, guides, teaches, comforts, and corrects us.

Praise God today for His wondrous works!

Read Ephesians 12:4
Lord, how marvelous is Your salvation.
Thank You!

Ultimate Freedom

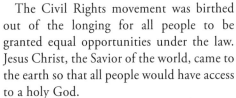

Let the freedom of the King rise among us.
LET IT RISE by Holland Davis

The Civil Rights movement was birthed out of the longing for all people to be granted equal opportunities under the law. Jesus Christ, the Savior of the world, came to the earth so that all people would have access to a holy God.

In Christ, there is neither slave nor free, foreigner nor local. In Christ, we are all one in the Spirit. God is no respecter of persons; He loves us all the same.

In Galatians 5, Paul teaches that through the work of the cross we are free, and he cautions us to never allow ourselves to be enslaved again. Regardless of our family or nationality, we are set free through the death of Christ. It is time to become empowered by His love. May His freedom reign in your heart today.

Read Galatians 5:1
I praise You, Lord, for freeing me from the bondage of sin.

Given Away

Willingly we choose to surrender our lives.
COME, NOW IS THE TIME TO WORSHIP by Brian Doerksen

We sometimes talk about giving ourselves away for the cause of Christ. Easy to say, harder to do. We'd rather just let God use us than to actually yield ourselves to Him. That way we can feel good, serve—do some good—but we don't have to submit or truly sacrifice. Submission and sacrifice are inconvenient, after all. They don't fit our agendas very well. But consider this: we might gain better use of our lives if we humbly submitted our hearts to God instead of raising our hands to do more tasks.

When we find it easier to get to work on time than to church, it's time to throw up our hands in surrender. When we don't make time to study our Bibles, pray, or worship, it's time to reprioritize. Contrary to popular belief, surrendering is a sign of strength, not weakness. In fact, it is the first step to worship.

Read Philippians 2:17
Lord, I surrender to You. Use me.

Coming Clean

Search me, O God, and know my heart today; try me, O Savior, know my thoughts, I pray.
CLEANSE ME by J. Edwin Orr

We call them excuses. Placing the blame where it belongs (on somebody else!). Little white lies. But the Bible calls these things sin. Unfortunately, we can so successfully hide our own sins from ourselves that we need God's help to search them out. Conviction is necessary, and confession is indeed good for the soul. Cleansing comes when we speak the truth and agree with God's Word; we admit, "You're right, God. I gossiped about my boss to my coworker today, and that's sin. Please forgive me."

Sure, God already knows the truth. But when we confess our splattered mud and water stains, He starts scrubbing the windows of our hearts until they let nothing through but clear sunlight. That's a real spring cleaning.

Read 1 John 1:9
Show me what's in my heart, Lord, so I can come clean with You.

Nature's Proof

Praise for the sweetness of the wet garden, sprung in completeness where His feet pass.
MORNING HAS BROKEN by Eleanor Farjeon

If you've ever lived in the northern climates, you know how invigorated you get at the first signs of spring after a cold, dormant winter. Grass turning from brown to green, birds singing, flowers and leaves reappearing—each one testifying that life is returning. It's amazing how the changing seasons bear witness to the life-giving power of our Creator God.

God engages our senses as He blesses us with life, beauty, and joy. In His goodness, He provides for and sustains His creation and His children. The earth reveals God's dominion through winter's bitter, cold dormancy, as well as spring's rebirth, summer's growth, and autumn's harvest. Each day His presence is evident in nature, as it is in our lives.

Focus your heart on God's blessings through His creation. Praise Him for everything you see and experience as a gift from Him.

Read John 1:3
I am awed by the beauty of Your creation, God.

Rescued

When He comes, our glorious King, all His ransomed home to bring,
then anew this song we'll sing, hallelujah, what a Savior!

MAN OF SORROWS, WHAT A NAME! by Philip P. Bliss

We see it in the movies and on television—suspenseful story lines that depict distraught parents or spouses ready to pay a huge ransom for the safe return of a kidnapped family member. Will they or won't they make the exchange? Can they trust that their loved one will be returned unharmed? It makes for good drama.

Jesus Christ, our glorious King, paid our ransom. He gave His life in exchange for the lives of undeserving, sinful people. Unrecognizable as royalty, Jesus was rejected, beaten, and humiliated. He took our place and became our Savior. He walked the earth because God's plan required Him to become a man and die in our place so that we could receive new life by faith. Let's give Him praise for overpowering the grave!

We have been ransomed. Jesus has secured our freedom from sin and the grave. He is our Savior.

Read Isaiah 53:1
For securing my salvation, Jesus, I will forever be grateful.

Best Deal in Town

Marvelous, infinite, matchless grace, freely bestowed on all who believe!
GRACE GREATER THAN OUR SIN by Julia H. Johnston

The advertisement read, "Free for first 30 days. It's easy. Just try it. After first 30 days you will be billed $34.95 per month unless you cancel your order. Offer valid for 24 hours." The product was not freely given—there was a cost after the first thirty days.

We have a reason to be thankful. God's matchless grace is freely given to all who place their faith in Him. For all time.

Without God, we cannot earn—nor do we deserve—a reprieve from our sin penalty. God's grace is amazing because it frees us from punishment and allows us to fellowship with Him eternally. His mercy has no "fine print" and it's a deal we truly can't refuse—nothing can compare to it.

If you have not received God's marvelous, infinite, matchless gift of free grace, place your faith and trust in Him today. After all, time is running out.

Read Romans 5:20
Dear God, thank You for Your unbelievably free gift of grace.

God's Story

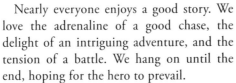

I heard an old, old story, how a Savior came from glory,
how He gave His life on Calvary to save a wretch like me.
Victory in Jesus by Eugene M. Bartlett

Nearly everyone enjoys a good story. We love the adrenaline of a good chase, the delight of an intriguing adventure, and the tension of a battle. We hang on until the end, hoping for the hero to prevail.

The Bible also tells a story. It holds all of the elements of an epic saga: treacherous betrayal, seemingly impossible romance, and a rescue mission. There is an evil villain to be destroyed and a Hero determined to do anything to save His imprisoned bride. However, because we're so familiar with the story, it's easy to grow passive about recommending it to family and friends who need its powerful message.

Take time to re-engage with the excitement of God's Word. Then "post" your review. Tell the people around you about the story that changed your life.

Read 1 Corinthians 15:57
Thank You, Lord, for giving us the Bible, so that we may read about Your hand in history.

Service with a Smile

When I stand in glory, I will see His face; there I'll serve my King forever in that holy place.
There Is a Redeemer by Melody Green

Seeing God—we can't even imagine just how awesome it will be. We'll finally be face-to-face with the Lover of our souls who has waited patiently to be united with us. Not that heaven will only be hours and hours of rapturous gazing at our Savior and King. Scripture tells us that we'll join a heavenly choir; we'll be reunited with loved ones; we'll eat and celebrate and sing praises to the King of glory. And we will have fulfilling, joyous work to do—work that thrills us and fits us and that we were uniquely created for.

Perhaps you see work as a daily grind today. You may watch the clock's hands ticking down the minutes, wishing for a career or position that better fulfills you. Or maybe your soul yearns for time off to enjoy rest and relaxation.

Rejoice! Today's drudgery or fatigue won't follow you to eternity. Tomorrow's work will have a purpose like you've never imagined. And you will be in your Father's magnificent presence. Forever.

Read Job 19:25
Lord, thank You for qualifying me for the best job ever.

Eternal Friend

He is our Guide and Friend; to us He'll condescend; His love shall never end.
COME, CHRISTIANS, JOIN TO SING by Christian H. Bateman

Mention the word condescend, and people instantly think of someone who patronizes another person or exhibits a spirit of superiority. Yet when our Savior "condescended" to live among us mortals, He lowered Himself—reduced Himself. He actually descended to our level, not in frustration but out of compassion. He humbly took the position of a natural man so He could serve as our guide.

Just as He was to the disciples, He is still our model today—an example of how we should carry ourselves in a hostile world. But He didn't stop there. Jesus was also a friend to all sinners, laying down His life for us. Just as He said in John 5, He sacrificed both His divine existence and His earthly life to bring us, His friends, hope.

As believers, we have reason to praise Him together for His supernatural love.

Read Psalm 150

Savior and Friend, thank You for loving me that much. Your love makes me worthy.

Ever-present Help

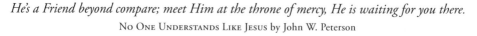

He's a Friend beyond compare; meet Him at the throne of mercy, He is waiting for you there.
No One Understands Like Jesus by John W. Peterson

On June 18, 2007, evangelist and faithful servant Billy Graham shared, "Ruth is my soulmate and best friend, and I cannot imagine living a single day without her by my side." Graham made the comment about his wife just one day before she died. After sixty-four years of marriage, they were truly life partners who journeyed through the decades together.

Just as Ruth was to Billy, many of us are fortunate to have had a trusted companion and confidant—one whose intentions are always the best. Yet there remain human limitations and inadequacies that keep every need from being met. Thankfully, our Savior is a friend beyond compare, never failing or lagging. He shows supernatural compassion, love, and understanding as He journeys with us through the hills and valleys of life. Christ is our constant companion, ready to answer even before we call.

Read Proverbs 18:24
I am privileged to have You walking side by side with me, Lord.

See No Evil

We turn our eyes from evil things; O Lord we cast down our idols.
GIVE US CLEAN HANDS by Charlie Hall

If you grew up going to church, chances are you learned a song with verses that warned, "Oh, be careful little eyes what you see; oh, be careful little ears what you hear...." Each verse ended with the reminder that our Father in heaven is paying attention, wanting us to choose wisely and walk only His path. Good lessons at any age.

For adults today, it's nearly impossible to escape the foul language, violent media images, false teachings of well-loved celebrities, and other cultural trappings. While we want to be accepted by our peers, we risk compromising our relationship with Christ if we try to meet their expectations. Only God can help us guard our hearts and minds. Turn your eyes and ears toward Him.

Read Psalm 24:3–6
Lord, keep me focused on the things that are pure and excellent—the things that please You.

Washed Clean

I see His love and mercy washing over all our sin. The people sing, the people sing.
HOSANNA by Brooke Fraser

Winters in the northern cities throughout the United States can be long and harsh. Beginning in November and continuing throughout the winter months, storms take their toll, and by the end of March, months of polluted snow piles up. When it begins to melt, it leaves behind the residue of salt, car exhaust, and mud. April showers are welcomed as they wash away the remains, cleanse sidewalks and streets, and bring life back to the slumbering foliage.

Praise God that when we place our faith and trust in Him, we gain access to the One who washes away the filth of our sin. Just as those cleansing rains bathe the earth, He makes us spotless and brings the hope of new life. News this good compels even the most tone-deaf among us to sing, because we have been blessed with forgiveness and granted a covering for sin.

Read Psalm 32:1–2
I ask, Lord, that You let Your mercy wash away my sins forever.

Sweetest Victory!

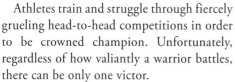

He's alive and I'm forgiven; heaven's gates are open wide.
HE'S ALIVE! by Don Francisco

Athletes train and struggle through fiercely grueling head-to-head competitions in order to be crowned champion. Unfortunately, regardless of how valiantly a warrior battles, there can be only one victor.

John's vision in Revelation 1 of our Messiah makes the soul tremble with joy. Verses 17–18 (NKJV) read: "And when I saw Him, I fell at His feet as dead. But He laid His right hand on me, saying to me, 'Do not be afraid; I am the First and the Last. I am He who lives, and was dead, and behold, I am alive forevermore. Amen. And I have the keys of Hades and of Death.'"

Sweet, sweet victory! Sin can no longer keep its stranglehold on our souls; Christ is alive and has conquered the enemy. By the power of His holy blood we are forgiven and heaven's gates are now open wide for us. Praise God, Jesus Christ is alive!

Read John 20:1–10
My Lord and God, thank You for making a way for me to have victory over sin and death!

Long-Term Satisfaction

Ponder nothing worldly minded, for with blessing in His hand
Christ our God to earth descendeth, our full homage to demand.

Let All Mortal Flesh Keep Silence by Gerard Moultrie

In the 1960s records were the way to listen to music. Enter the seventies, and it was eight-track tapes. From there we moved to cassettes to CDs and MP3 players. What may be popular today likely already has a replacement coming.

This world is temporary. Nothing lasts for long. Yet people strive to keep up with the latest trends. We want to appear as if we've got it together, that we're on top of the latest and greatest. We'll even go into debt to accomplish that goal.

Thankfully, the provisions of Christ are eternal. And through Him alone we can know true and lasting blessing, peace, joy, life, and hope. Nothing in this world even begins to compare to the contentment found in Him. He is our response to the lure of temptations that result in short-lived gratification.

Praise Him! There is nothing in this world that can satisfy your soul. But He is able.

Read Habakkuk 2:20

Jesus, You and Your blessings are everlasting.
I honor You.

Defy the Odds

Faith of our fathers, living still, in spite of dungeon, fire, and sword.
FAITH OF OUR FATHERS by Frederick W. Faber

Every senior at Englewood's Urban Prep School for young men in Chicago, Illinois, is college bound. The African-American, all-male school successfully met its mission—100 percent of its students were accepted into a four-year college. Despite the odds and in the midst of poverty, gangs, unemployment, teen pregnancy, and staggering high school dropout rates, these students reached their goal and are confident of a bright future ahead.

In God we have a faith that is not dependent upon this world or the odds stacked against us. Our faith is based on who God is—our Creator, Sustainer, Provider—the One who can do anything but fail! Like Abraham, Daniel, and Joseph before us, we believe in God, despite our circumstances. By faith, we too can believe the impossible is possible.

Read Jude 1:3
Help me to live by faith today, precious Savior!

Immeasurable Love

To write the love of God above, would drain the ocean dry.
The Love of God by F. M. Lehman

Before a mother has even seen her baby, she feels connected to it. She and the child are bonded. And when she holds that baby for the first time, adoration is what surges through her heart.

Sadly, for many of us, past hurts make us skeptical about what it means to truly be loved and give love. Pain has left a chasm so wide inside us that it's hard to even relate to a loving God. Yet millions of hurting souls have come to know Jesus as Lord and Savior and can testify that God's love "goes beyond the highest star and reaches to the lowest hell." His love soothes, heals, and renews our hearts.

In Him, we find a love even more intense than a new mother's. The love of God is pure, measureless, and strong. And no one or nothing can deprive us of it.

Read 1 John 3:1
Your boundless love is strength, O God.

Eternal Perspective

Hail, Abraham's God and mine! I join the heavenly lays;
all might and majesty are Thine and endless praise.
THE GOD OF ABRAHAM, PRAISE! by Thomas Olivers

Next time you're up in an airplane, choose the window seat. Note how the landscape changes as you take off and then gain altitude. Massive buildings become tiny. Fertile fields are transformed into a quilt of green patchwork squares. From this perspective, you can see where roads divide and intersect. But on the ground, where you have a limited perspective, you can only see what's right before your eyes.

Now consider God's perspective. He sees every aspect of our lives—not only the physical, but the emotional, mental, and spiritual too.

He keeps in mind what has happened in the past, and He knows what lies ahead.

The Eternal has always existed. He is the God who spoke to Moses on Mount Sinai and appeared to Paul on the Damascus road. He is the God who promised Abraham that his descendants would be as numerous as the stars, and the God who set those stars in space. He is the God who whispers in our ears today.

Read Romans 4:18–20
Lord, help me to see my life, my circumstances,
and the people around me from Your perspective.

Christ's Provision

It's washed away, all my sin and all my shame.
JESUS PAID IT ALL by Alex Nifong, Elvina M. Hall, and John Thomas Grape

Scripture is clear. Not only have we all sinned and come short of God's glory, the penalty for those sins is death. Death is not just a physical end but also a spiritual, resulting in eternal separation from our Creator. We were lost, hopeless, with no possibility of salvation or rescue from punishment. Yet God, in His compassion, graciously provided His only son as payment. Upon His death, the account was paid up and closed out.

It is through the blood of Christ that we are redeemed, forgiven, justified, and sanctified. We now have access to God and can stand before Him free from the burden and shame of sin. Jesus made it possible for us to be not just accepted but welcomed into eternal fellowship with our heavenly Father.

Have you accepted Christ's provision for sin? Today can be your day of salvation!

Read 2 Corinthians 5:21
What a sacrifice You made on my behalf, Lord Jesus!

Let's Dance

You are my strong melody. You are my dancing rhythm.
YOU ARE SO GOOD TO ME by Don Chaffer, Ben Pasley, and Robin Pasley

The book of Psalms has a lot to say about music and dance. In fact, David demonstrated this form of praise when the Ark of the Covenant was returned to Jerusalem. Many of David's psalms praise the Lord for His grace, for turning His people's mourning into dancing, and for bringing songs to their lips. The Bible depicts dancing as a pure expression of joy.

When we are feeling low, singing and dancing may be the last activities we want to do! Yet it is in times of hurt and distress that we should seek God's face through Scripture and also be open to the hope that is so often conveyed through song. He can use the gift of praise and worship music to lift a burdened spirit.

Allow God to give you the melody that will make you want to dance—regardless of what you face.

Read Psalm 149:3
O God, You are the song in my heart and my dance of joy!

Clean Slate

*There is a fountain filled with blood drawn from Immanuel's veins,
and sinners plunged beneath that flood lose all their guilty stains.*

THERE IS A FOUNTAIN FILLED WITH BLOOD by William Cowper

Two teenagers were caught robbing and vandalizing a family-owned, neighborhood corner store. Property was damaged and inventory was lost. The owners pressed charges against the students and the court handed down its judgment—requiring them to perform community service to help restore what had been damaged. Yet some of the lingering hurt and loss couldn't be fixed with a paint brush, hammer, or mop—there was also a personal loss of trust and sense of security.

In contrast, Jesus, as the perfect sacrificial Lamb, paid the price and satisfied our sin liability in full. In our corrupted state, there was nothing good that we could have done to pay the debt owed to God. His perfect sacrifice freed humanity from the required penalty of death. Because of it, the breech between us has been healed and our relationship with a holy God totally restored.

Read Romans 5:8–9

Because Your blood has given me a clean slate, Jesus, I have a fresh start today.

Mirror His Passion

Father...Jesus...Spirit, we love You, we worship and adore You.
GLORIFY THY NAME by Donna Adkins

The boy followed the words on the screen and sang along as best he could. The pews were filled with many others like him—standing at attention, adding their voices to the music, but their bodies were stiff. A gentle swaying was the most radical motion in sight, and the boy was acutely aware of it. Uncomfortable, he felt compelled to do something—anything—so he threw his hands up in the air and closed his eyes until the end of the song. To his surprise, by the time he opened them, others were candidly worshiping, unrestrained.

One of the greatest inhibitors of public worship is our fear of self-expression. The question of what others will think of us tends to distract from genuine adoration. But take a look at King David's ways of worship in the Old Testament. His life is testament to the fact that no half-hearted devotion will do in our relationship with God. Our Creator will take undignified praise over a lukewarm response any day.

Read John 12:28
Father, let nothing inhibit me as I worship You.

Jesus Is There

Hallelujah, He is coming. Hallelujah, He is here.
I Looked Up, author unknown

Looking for Jesus? You're not the only one. There were many in the Bible who looked for Him too. His parents, Joseph and Mary, lost Him in the temple when He was twelve. His followers sought Him out when they were hungry. The women searched for Him, only to find an empty grave.

Fortunately, Jesus is never lost. He is ever present, God with us, always where He promised to be. We may sometimes get lost, but He never does.

Do you want to know where He is right now? Jesus is at the right hand of God, interceding for you. Seek and you will find Him. Every time.

Read 1 Corinthians 15:22
You never lose Your way, Jesus. Keep me close to You.

Godly Perspective

He is Lord of heaven, Lord of earth; He is Lord of all who live.
He is Lord above the universe; all praise to Him we give.

WE WILL GLORIFY by Twila Paris

Everything in life is a matter of perspective. While to us humans a cat is a small pet, consider the view from the mouse hole. For a freshman college student, a twelve-page research paper seems epic, yet for a seasoned author it's "chapter one of twenty." To a marathon runner, a 5K race may be just a warm-up, but to the person who hasn't exercised in years, it's an all-day event.

And so it goes with our spiritual journey. Faced with the reality of our sin and our weakness to temptation, we may feel over-whelmed, but it's nothing that God hasn't seen before. Where we anticipate inevitable defeat, He sees an opportunity for resounding victory over the enemy. Where we forecast discouragement, He plans comfort we've never imagined. So seek the mind of Christ about whatever you're facing—illness, loss, disappointment, relationship challenges. Ask God to open your eyes to the bigger picture—and praise Him for His ability to bring His plans to life.

Read Revelation 5:13
Thank You, Lord, for always having the bigger picture in sight.

Weak Made Strong

It is You, Lord, who knows my weakness, Who gives me strength with Thine own hand.
SANCTUARY by John W. Thompson and Randy Scruggs

In most job interviews, applicants are asked to identify their strengths and weaknesses. It's always a fine line, though, because if we are forthright about our weaknesses, we might jeopardize our chances of being chosen. On the flip side, talking too much about our strengths may come across as arrogant. The key to answering the interview question is to be candid but positive.

We'd do well to take a similar approach when we come before God. The difference is, He already knows us—He is well acquainted with our strengths and weaknesses—so there is no risk in our honesty. We can be frank with Him, asking Him to help us grow in ways He would be proud of. In return, He promises that His grace will be sufficient for us and that His power is perfected in our frailty; that when we are weak, He is strong.

Read Psalm 139:23–24

Search me, God, and know my heart.

Soul Provision

I take, O cross, thy shadow for my abiding place.
BENEATH THE CROSS OF JESUS by Elizabeth C. Clephane

Being a parent is an awesome responsibility. Good parents provide comfort and reassurance to their children. When a child becomes ill, Mommy or Daddy is the name that rings out in the middle of the night. Good parents offer a safe place for their children. Beneath their "wings" is a place of refuge and unconditional love.

It seems a contradiction that a painful cross could be such a refuge. But that is precisely the reality at the foot of Jesus's cross. There, no matter what burden you are bearing, you can find sympathy, grace, love, and mercy. In the shadow of His cross, your spirit will be calmed, your heart comforted, your will subdued, your soul strengthened.

Read John 19:25

Heavenly Father, thank You for the cross—a place of healing, redemption, sacrifice, grace, mercy, and strength!

February 22

Restored

What restores our faith in God, what reveals the Father's love?
Mighty Is the Power of the Cross by Chris Tomlin, Shawn Craig, and Jesse Reeves

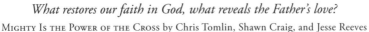

When we fall back into sinful behaviors that we thought we had left behind, our fellowship with God is immediately interrupted. Even after we repent and choose to return to righteous living and continue to move forward with our life in Christ, the feeling of distance from God sometimes lingers. The connection that was once so sweet now seems foreign, and our faith in our loving heavenly Father begins to falter. How can it be restored?

The book of Hebrews shows us that our merciful and compassionate High Priest, Jesus, perpetually offers Himself on our behalf as the perfect sacrifice. His blood not only inaugurated our salvation but keeps purifying and sanctifying us—forever and ever. His voluntary death on the cross reveals the Father's unfaltering love, not just the first time we avail ourselves of it but every time our faith weakens and needs restoring.

Are you missing an intimacy with God? Look no farther than the cross.

Read Hebrews 10:10–17
God, I believe Your Word more than my feelings.

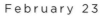

The Will of God

I am not skilled to understand what God has willed, what God has planned.
MY SAVIOR, MY GOD by Aaron Shust and Dorothy Dora Greenwell

People often speak of the will of God in vague terms, as though it is some strange mystery that can never really be understood. However, nothing could be further from the truth.

Careful study of the Bible clearly presents His will for us. God created us in His own image and for a very specific purpose: that He would be glorified and that His kingdom would be advanced. Through Jesus, God made it possible for us to have an intimate relationship with Him.

How are you demonstrating that relationship, that commitment to Him? If you start to get discouraged, remember: He has provided you with the tools you need to carry out His will. You have His Word, so that you can know what He wants; His Holy Spirit to guide you as you do His work; and the marvelous provision of prayer in order to have constant access to Him. You are equipped to fulfill His purpose!

Read Romans 12:2
Father God, I ask that You empower my life so that I can walk in Your will and Your way.

Yes, I Am Able

Lord, we are able—our spirits are Thine. Remold them, make us like Thee, divine.
Are Ye Able, Said the Master by Earl Marlatt

In Auschwitz, the Nazi death camp, ten men were sentenced to death by starvation as punishment for the escape of another prisoner. One of the men cried out, asking that he be permitted to live for his family's sake. Upon hearing that plea, a priest named Maximilian Kolbe volunteered to take the man's place. He died two weeks later as a result of this sacrifice.

Most of us cannot imagine being brave enough to make such a sacrifice. Kolbe, however, had been following God since childhood and allowed the Lord to mold his spirit for many years. He was able to say, "Lord, I am able"—able to serve, able to love, able to give even his life.

If we allow God to shape our spirits, we too will be prepared to say, "Lord, we are able," in reply to whatever He asks of us.

Are you able?

Read Isaiah 29:16
Mold my spirit, Lord, so that I will always serve You.

Space for Grace

O come to my heart, Lord Jesus; there is room in my heart for Thee.
Thou Didst Leave Thy Throne by Emily E. S. Elliott

We make room for all kinds of things in our lives: TV shows, movies, online surfing, social networking, work, spouse, family—and maybe a little church now and then. We create time in our schedules for leisure reading and yard work and vacations and coffee with friends. But in our daily calendars, is there space for the Lord? Even more importantly, is there any room for Him in our hearts?

Surely there is room in our hearts for the One who did so much for us. Certainly there is room in our hearts for the One who sacrificed Himself to deliver us from ourselves.

As you're planning your calendar for this upcoming week, why not schedule a few appointments with the Lord? Then plan for that time like you would a visit with a friend. You won't regret it. Making space for Him will do wonders for your heart.

Read John 1:11
I would like to meet with You, Jesus, and get a little time just to ourselves.

Live by Faith

Lord, hurry the day when our faith shall be sight.
Lord Jesus, Come by Adam Sacks

Let's face it: we spend a big percentage of our day slugging through life's challenges. It's not easy to reflect the Father's light when circumstances leave us battling for a positive attitude.

In tough times, we must turn away from the mounting irritations that hinder us and turn toward the impending appearance of Jesus. Because in time He will make everything right. Everything.

Living in anticipation of His return is only proper. Paul, Peter, John—virtually all the New Testament writers—lived hopefully, expecting with joy and certainty that one day they would see Jesus break through the clouds. It is a wonderful example of how we should live now. At His return, He will right all wrongs, heal all diseases, and pour everlasting joy on all who trust in Him and have been waiting for His promised return. In the meantime, we live with confident hope that we will one day see Him face-to-face, and our faith will truly become sight.

Read 1 Peter 1:8–9
Dear Jesus, help us to face difficulties with the remembrance that one day, You will return and right all wrongs.

Jesus Christ, the True Superstar

One more day, and it's not the same, Your Spirit calls my heart to sing.
All I Need Is You by Marty Sampson

Seeing celebrities is exciting. Especially when magazines and television shows allow us to peek inside their daily lives. On the rare chance we get to see celebrities in person, we rush to tell our friends and relatives. We feel lucky when we encounter important people.

God is greater than any celebrity figure. Seeing Him in the person of Jesus Christ must have been fascinating. For a while, Christ's contemporaries treated Him like a celebrity. Large crowds came to hear His teachings and followed Him from town to town. They hung on His every word and crowded into any room in which He sat down. Talk about groupies!

But as He approached the cross, most of His closest followers fell away and disowned Him. It was only after the resurrection that they discovered the true implications of His life and teaching.

When we see Jesus for who He truly is, our lives are changed forever, and we cannot help but sing His praises.

Read Acts 4:20
Thank You, Lord, for changing us with Your love.

Perfect Love

You came from heaven to earth to show the way.
Lord I Lift Your Name on High by Rick Founds

Genesis tells the story of how sin entered the world through Satan's lies and Adam and Eve's choices. Because of His righteousness, God brought judgment on all mankind. Yet in His loving-kindness, He mercifully provided us with a way out. Our God "became flesh" to satisfy our greatest need—redemption that allowed us back into full fellowship with Him.

Jesus left His home in glory to enter a world full of hurt and lies, bringing truth and becoming the living sacrifice for our sins. It was only God's perfect and holy Son that could cleanse and rescue all of us.

Our Savior modeled the love He wanted each of us to embrace and show one another. It's an unselfish love, one that sees beyond race, gender, and class. A love that proclaims, "Your needs are more important than my desires."

Read John 6:38
Jesus, You are my example for living.

March 1

Just Passing Through

What rejoicing in His presence when are banished grief and pain,
when the crooked ways are straightened and the dark things shall be plain.
FACE TO FACE by Carrie E. Breck

On January 12, 2010, the worst earthquake in more than two hundred years struck Haiti. Twelve aftershocks followed the devastating quake that left more than 300,000 people dead and displaced millions. In the midst of the homelessness and devastation, the death toll continued to rise. Photographers captured the grief, pain, and destruction that plagued the country.

Jesus desires to give us comfort and rest in the midst of our sorrows, and He promises to bring peace to all who will place their faith in Him. Although grief and pain will come, Jesus is a friend who sticks closer than a brother.

This world is a temporary experience for us; we do not have to endure its pain and devastation forever. When you stand before God, there will be no more sorrow and tribulation. No more tears. Only peace. Only joy. Forever.

Read 1 Corinthians 13:12
Dear Father, I am overwhelmed by the joy and peace I experience in Your presence, even here on earth.

He Gave Everything

That's why we bow down and worship this King 'cause He gave His everything.
THAT'S WHY WE PRAISE HIM by Tommy Walker

Imagine the king of a great and prosperous country stepping down from his throne… for a homeless person. Not only does he give up his throne, he abandons his palace, his comfortable lifestyle, beautiful clothes, and delicious food, and becomes a poor man. A man with no place to lay his head and no possessions. Then imagine this man offering to save your life. Offering to sacrifice himself in order to come to your rescue.

We don't have to imagine it at all. There is one King in the history of the world that did this for us, and His sacrifice is why He deserves our worship. When we bow before Him, we know He is worthy of our praise.

Jesus gave His everything—and became nothing—so that we might step into life eternal.

Read Philippians 2:5–8
I will worship You, Lord, because of what You gave so that I might live.

A True Friend

He bled, He died to save me; and not alone the gift of life, but His own self He gave me.
I've Found a Friend, O Such a Friend by James G. Small

What's the difference between an acquaintance and a true friend? An acquaintance is someone you see casually every now and then, or someone with whom you never get beyond the surface. A true friend is by your side in good times and in bad. Someone you can call no matter how late it is. Someone who will sacrifice their own schedule or convenience to come to your aid. Someone who goes deep with you.

True, selfless friends are hard to come by. Times of adversity reveal who our true friends are. The good news is, you never have to wonder with Jesus; He is always a friend. A friend to those who feel friendless—the Companion who endures with you through loss and sadness. In fact, He is more than a friend—He is Savior and Lord.

Friendships will come and go, but a relationship with Christ will last forever.

Read Proverbs 17:17

Jesus, You are a Friend who sticks closer than a brother. That is my comfort.

Promised Paradise

My heart can sing when I pause to remember, a heartache here is but a stepping stone.
UNTIL THEN by Stuart Hamblen

The Bible speaks of a new heaven and a new earth, where God will dwell with his people, where He will personally "wipe away every tear from their eyes; there shall be no more death, nor sorrow, nor crying. There shall be no more pain, for the former things have passed away" (Revelation 21:4 NKJV).

It's hard to imagine, isn't it? A place so perfect, where life and love and joy abound without any shadow of concern. It's especially hard to imagine when the cares and troubles of this life are all-consuming. But be encouraged. God's Word assures us that this earthly life is only temporary. A new day is coming; the disappointments of this life are short-term. The Alpha and Omega—the Beginning and the End—will bring all that He promised to fruition, and we will live forever with Him.

Until then, we can rejoice that this old world is not our final home.

Read Psalm 63:3
Thanks for Your promises of a new heaven and a new earth, God!

White as Snow

Lord Jesus, I long to be perfectly whole; I want Thee forever to live in my soul.
Break down every idol, cast out every foe.

Whiter Than Snow by James L. Nicholson

Watching the pristine white snow fall from the sky and blanket the earth can be a breathtaking experience. It only takes a few days, however, for that same pure-white snow to become polluted and dirty. And once things start to melt, those once-beautiful snow banks become hills of cold, hard mud.

It's not too different from the effects of sin in our lives. Initially the change is barely noticeable, but in time, sin corrupts us completely.

Thankfully, God bleaches away our stain with Jesus's precious blood. He can make us clean again when we invite Him to take up residence in our souls. Invited in, He destroys every idol in our lives and casts out anything that gets in the way of our service.

King David knew what it was to have sin creep into his life, and he pleaded with God—asking Him to renew his spirit and cleanse his heart. Will you pray that prayer today?

Read Psalm 51:7
Search me. Forgive me. Cleanse me.

Good God Almighty

People from every nation and tongue, from generation to generation, we worship You.
You Are Good by Israel Houghton

God is good all the time. Yes, all the time. He provided a ram, sparing Abraham the pain of sacrificing his son Isaac. He closed the mouths of the lions when Daniel was cast into the den. He used a boy with perilously little food to feed the thousands who came to hear Jesus preach. He sent Jesus to bear our sin when we were not capable.

All the time, God is good. Capable of turning back invading armies, ending droughts, drying up floods, bringing about vast harvests. And you could certainly add to the list...

In light of the truth, in light of His overwhelming generosity toward us, we have no choice but to bow down and worship the God of all gods—above us, beyond us, beside us, and inside us—our good, good God.

Read Psalm 100:5
Your goodness and mercy to me are beyond compare.

The Ransom Price

My chains are gone, I've been set free. My God, my Savior has ransomed me.
AMAZING GRACE (MY CHAINS ARE GONE) by Chris Tomlin, Louie Giglio, and John Newton

In "The Ransom of Red Chief" by O. Henry, two scalawags kidnap the only son of a wealthy citizen in a small Alabama town, hoping to extract a large ransom. The boy, however, turns out to be a mischievous prankster whom no one wants back. Not even the boy's father wants to pay the ransom.

Humankind, too, was kidnapped and held for ransom. We were prisoners to sin and Satan, with no way to free ourselves. Considering our selfish human nature, no one should have been willing to pay our ransom. We needed a Savior. Thankfully, the Creator God loved us—rescuing and redeeming our lives through the sacrifice of His Son.

Because of Jesus's death, the chains of sin and death no longer have power over us—our ransom has been paid and we are free.

Read Hebrews 9:14–15
Jesus, thank You for paying my ransom.

Fountain of Life

All who are weak, come to the fountain.
All Who Are Thirsty by Brenton Brown

The soft, rustling sound of moving water is therapeutic. Most spas use fountains to create an atmosphere that alleviates stress and calms customers. There is even a component of "fountain therapy" that claims it can relieve depression, help alcoholics stay sober, and allow pregnant women to have healthy deliveries. Fountains provide peace and tranquility for tired, weary people.

When Christ dined at Matthew's house for the first time, the Pharisees were astonished by His actions. They didn't understand why an important, spiritual man like Jesus would spend His time with sinners and tax collectors.

But Jesus came for the sick, not the healthy. Like a fountain of life, He came to help those who struggle and heal those who hurt. When we draw near to Christ, we are comforted by the sweet sounds of His unmitigated, limitless love. He is our Living Water.

Feeling weak? Come today and refresh yourself at the fountain.

Read Matthew 9:12–13
I come to Your fountain of redemption, Jesus, asking you to refresh me and make me new.

The Full Trinity

All praise and thanks to God the Father now be given, the Son,
and Him who reigns with them in highest heaven.
NOW THANK WE ALL OUR GOD by Martin Rinkart

The concept of the Trinity is a familiar one in Christianity. We pray to God as our heavenly Father and to Jesus as our Savior. Often, however, the Holy Spirit gets overlooked.

Yet in Scripture, when the Spirit acted or came to rest upon someone, powerful things happened. In the Old Testament, the power of the Spirit caused men to prophesy and Israel's enemies to fall. In the New Testament, people were healed, truth was revealed, and souls turned from darkness to light.

The Holy Spirit should not be forgotten or left out. Jesus told His followers—and, therefore, us—that we would receive power from the Spirit. He convicts and encourages us, empowering our faith walk.

When we praise God and thank Him for what He does, let us remember to honor Him for all He is—Father, Son, and Spirit.

Read Matthew 28:19
Thank You, Lord, for all that You are—
Father, Son, and Holy Spirit.

Our Rock

O safe to the Rock that is higher than I, my soul in its conflicts and sorrows would fly.
HIDING IN THEE by William O. Cushing

The "fight or flight syndrome" is a response to sudden danger. Our bodies release adrenaline that causes our hearts to beat faster; because of that, more oxygen goes to our muscles.

Suddenly our brain is alert and focused on the danger at hand. The result is an urge to fight or run. If the imminent danger can lead to bodily harm, our immediate response may be flight. After all, self-preservation is a natural instinct.

God, our Rock, offers eternal safety and security. With Him, we don't have to defend ourselves or worry about self-preservation.

God is dependable, unchangeable, and constant; He offers a haven to which we can flee. In the midst of an unsafe relationship, unstable job situation, or volatile economy, He is the place where our souls can find rest. He is the mountain that provides protection for the believer, the truth in the midst of confusion and conflict. How blessed we are!

If you feel overwhelmed by conflicts and sorrows, call on God today.

Read Psalm 62:6
In Your refuge and strength, Father, I find peace.

Like a River

Joys are flowing like a river since the Comforter has come.
BLESSED QUIETNESS by Manie P. Ferguson

Rivers begin in mountains or hills, fed by underground springs or runoff from snowmelt or rain. Then, as they move, they grow larger and gain momentum—collecting water from smaller streams along the way. At times, the influx of water pushes rivers to a level that overflows their banks. Other times it wanes as summer's heat builds, and slows to little more than a creek.

But the joy of the Lord never wanes. Just like a mighty river continuously flows through the landscape, so do the blessings of the Holy Spirit surge within us. Our Comforter refreshes and cleanses us with divine understanding and peace, regardless of what we face.

In the midst of life's noise, confusion, and concerns, we can experience serenity through the Comforter; He is always with us. Continual blessings flow because the Comforter speaks to us and through us. Because He leads and guides us, we have joys that flow like a river.

Read John 14:16
Dear God, thank You for the provision of peace that can only come from You.

Take My Life

I honor You, I worship You, oh Lord.
WORTHY IS THE LAMB by Carl Tuttle

We host dinners in honor of heroes. We honor celebrities for their artistic accomplishments. Students with superior grades are listed on the honor roll. In showing our admiration and respect for hard work, we exalt those who deserve our respect.

Who is more worthy of our reverence than our Savior, Jesus Christ? He willingly gave up His heavenly place—not for earthly recognition and stature but to be betrayed, rejected, and persecuted. Even though He healed the sick and fed the hungry, the people ultimately shouted, "Crucify Him!"

What should He receive from us? As King of kings and our champion over death, He is worthy of all honor, all gratitude, all praise. Jesus is worthy of a life dedicated to His service. That is how we exalt Him.

Read Psalm 100:2
Here I am to worship You, Lord. Accept my offering.

The Best Is Yet to Come

Face to face in all of His glory.
We Shall Behold Him by Dottie Rambo

Have you heard the story of the woman diagnosed with a terminal illness who wished to determine her funeral arrangements? In meeting with her pastor, the woman selected the songs she wanted sung and the scriptures she wanted read. Then, as they finished their meeting, she added, "There's one more thing, Pastor. I want to be buried with a spoon in my right hand."

"Why a spoon?" the pastor asked.

"You see," she replied, "every Sunday after worship, I serve in the church's kitchen. And as we are serving the main course we always tell people, 'Make sure you keep your spoon.' Why? Because after the main course comes dessert. As people file by my casket and wonder about the spoon, I want you to remind them that I've finished my main course and kept my spoon because the best is yet to come!"

The blessing of salvation is the best yet-to-come that we could be given. All believers will one day be face-to-face with our Savior. So hang on to your spoon! You have so much more to look forward to!

Read Revelation 1:7
Precious Lord, the hope of eternity spurs me on.

Reflecting the Light

Oh, that we could reflect You, show You to the world that You love.
PRICELESS TREASURE by Charlie Hall

The world doesn't need more people who shine brightly for a while in their own achievements, their own looks, their own abilities. We've had our fill of temporary idols, haven't we?

What we need are people we recognize not for their own accomplishments but because they brightly reflect God's beauty and love. Such people are more like the moon than stars, for the moon only shines because it reflects the light of the sun.

That's the beauty of the gospel: that God would choose imperfect, broken people like us to reflect His light in a dark world. Let's stop worrying about building up a good image of ourselves in front of others. Instead, let's turn our eyes to Jesus and let Him love the world through us.

In what ways might you reflect Jesus's light into your world today?

Read Daniel 12:3
Reveal to me how I can reflect You today, God. That is my desire.

Friend for Life

He's my Savior, Messiah, Redeemer and Friend.
You Are Holy (Prince of Peace) by Marc Imboden and Tammi Rhoton

Who's your "BFF"—that special person who is supposed to be your best friend forever?

Because the term friend is often defined by people's actions and words, the "forever" part doesn't always hold. True friends, however, rise above the petty problems. They find ways to negotiate difficult situations, resolving conflict rather than letting it build. They genuinely enjoy hanging out together, learning about one another's thoughts, beliefs, and passions. They support each other through thick and thin. They add joy to each other's life.

Jesus is more than a friend. He is the best Friend we could ask for! One who sacrificed His own life so that ours could be saved. Praise Him today for His holy ways that make Him the Friend we didn't even know we could ask for—the Best BFF possible.

Read Proverbs 18:24
Jesus, thank You for being the Friend who sticks closer than a brother.

No Turning Back

The Cross before me, the world behind, no turning back.
Not to Us by Jesse Reeves and Chris Tomlin

Following Jesus does not come with a "thirty-day trial" clause like an Internet purchase or an insurance policy. Following Jesus is for keeps.

When Jesus told His disciples to pick up their crosses and follow Him, it was not just a figure of speech. Many of Jesus's earliest followers followed in His footsteps, right up to their own personal crosses. And though few Christians in the Western world have known martyrdom in recent centuries, the slaughter of believers elsewhere has not stopped.

In North America, generations of Jesus's followers may yet have to come to grips with life or death choices that regularly face our brothers and sisters in the rest of the world. We do not know what the future will hold, other than our God will be with us. But we need to decide now that we will follow Jesus right to—and through—the end.

Read Luke 9:23

I'm Yours, Lord. No turning back. Make me faithful!

Unlimited

Great is the Lord, He is faithful and true; by His mercy He proves He is love.
Great Is the Lord by Michael W. Smith and Deborah D. Smith

Greatness can be defined in a variety of ways—from quantity and size to celebrity and significance to power and influence. Yet try and define the greatness of our God. He embodies every synonym for greatness—and manages to exceed each one at the same time. He is immense, famous, noble, wonderful, huge, absolute, and important.

He is Lord of all—ruling powerfully. He embodies truth, faithfulness, and honor. Look around; as Creator, He is vast and limitless. In His holy and just nature, He is absolute. Thankfully, He is also loving and merciful beyond all measure.

Aren't you relieved that the God you serve is beyond what you could ask for or imagine? Spread the word! Our God is more than sufficient.

Read Psalm 19:1–3
You are the Rock on which I can stand. How great You are!

Strength in Weakness

Give us Your strength, O God, and courage to speak.
Perform Your wondrous deeds through those who are weak.
LET YOUR KINGDOM COME by Bob Kauflin

What makes us fragile? Our humanity? Our sinfulness? Our limitations—time, money, intelligence? People imagine conquering human weaknesses and limitations by creating superheroes, magicians, and even time-travel scenarios.

Numerous books and movie series depict average people rising up to save the world from wickedness; we imagine our ordinary selves in those heroes' extraordinary circumstances, conquering all.

Why do we neglect to include God in the equation? We can overcome by choosing to lean on His strength—allowing Him to be the one to defeat the enemy. Agree that vengeance is His, not ours. Let love cover a multitude of sins. Prayerfully allow the fruit of the Holy Spirit in us to triumph over evil.

When you are weak, then you are strong.

Read 2 Corinthians 12:9–10
God, may Your strength work through my weakness to accomplish Your eternal good.

God's Glory

To see You high and lifted up, shining in the light of Your glory.
OPEN THE EYES OF MY HEART, LORD by Paul Baloche

Who among us wouldn't like to have a chance to see God— even for a moment? Almost three thousand years ago a man named Isaiah did see the Lord. He saw Him "high and lifted up" (Isaiah 6:1 NKJV), surrounded by seraphim praising His name. And Isaiah was terrified. In that moment, seeing God for who He really was, Isaiah was forced to see himself for who he truly was.

Are you asking God to allow you to see Him, to know Him better today? Be prepared to catch a glimpse of your own wretched state! But then, get ready to bask in the fresh realization that Christ has taken away your guilt and that you can now come before God unashamed. Knowing you have been cleansed, you can take your eyes off yourself and lift them high to gaze upon God's glory.

Read Isaiah 6:1–7
God, give me a fresh understanding of who You really are.

No Cause for Despair

In all the world around me I see His loving care,
and though my heart grows weary, I never will despair.
HE LIVES by Alfred H. Ackley

One doesn't have to read much beyond the news headlines to find plenty of reasons to lose hope. There is so much heartache, destruction, and brokenness out there. It's no wonder our hearts grow weary.

Yet, dear friend, take a closer look, for the stories are steeped in redemption. What alarm did God sound that awoke the father of three so he could rush his family safely out of their burning home? While they were left with only the clothes on their backs, how thankful they were to have escaped. What alerted the officer to impending danger when he stopped to pull a mother and child from a broken-down van just moments before it exploded? What was the glimmer of hope that a young girl clung to when she decided to resist addiction—even though her own mother was strung out on drugs?

God's loving care is present in the desperation of every painful story. As surely as darkness abounds, His light and mercy abound still more. Sometimes it's just a little harder to see.

Read Matthew 28:7
Dear God, help me to see beyond the surface of people's stories to Your love and hope.

March 21

Let the Son Shine In

I ask no other sunshine than the sunshine of His face.
BENEATH THE CROSS OF JESUS by Elizabeth C. Clephane

We do what we can to endure winter's chill and gray—sun lamps, vacations to warm climates, tanning beds—but nothing restores us like the return of spring. Those warm, sunny days invigorate us, revitalize us, refresh us—and suddenly everything seems new again. There's just no substitute for the sun.

Scripture reminds us that there could be no substitute for Jesus either. There was no other acceptable alternative for humanity than the Son of God's supreme sacrifice.

His resurrection made a way for us to be children of the light. His love makes our joy and contentment possible, brightening even the harshest days with a hope that does not fade.

Read 1 John 4:12
Because You shine within me, Son of God, I never am without hope.

Brand-New

For the wonder of each hour of the day and of the night,
hill and vale and tree and flower, sun and moon and stars of light.
For the Beauty of the Earth by Folliot S. Pierpoint

The changing of every season is a miracle to behold, but perhaps none is as impressive as the transition from winter to spring. The dormant landscape starts to awaken. Desolate patches of hard ground erupt into rivers of bright flowers and verdant trees. Birds gather twigs to build their nests. Squirrels come out of hiding. The expanse of the sky, the smell of freshly cut grass, the feel of a warm breeze soaking across your skin—each and every vignette testifies to the breathtaking beauty of our world and God's creative power.

But His wondrous works don't end there.

He brings us through the personal seasons of life too, awakening our souls from spiritual darkness, providing fresh opportunities for growth. Consider today the miracles He's wrought in your life—the once-dry patches of your heart that now thrive because of His goodness. Thank God, He makes all things new!

Read Genesis 1:31
This is the day You have made; I shall rejoice and be glad in it!

Essential Camaraderie

We are not divided, all one body we—one in hope and doctrine, one in charity.
ONWARD CHRISTIAN SOLDIERS by Sabine Baring-Gould

What's more important to a body's function, the brain or the heart? If you had to choose, would you rather have a great set of lungs or two healthy kidneys? These questions seem impossible to answer; thankfully, we don't have to. God miraculously created the human body and its many working parts to perform together, each function supporting another.

Likewise, the body of Christ is best deployed as a unit, pressing forward in faith to accomplish the will of God. No single church, missionary, or ministry is more valuable than the next in God's economy.

Instead, we can be grateful for our differences of calling, conviction, and culture; each of these attributes allows us a chance to achieve great things for God's glory.

Ask the Father today what role He wants you to play and how that role interacts with others. Then, watch how together—as the body of Christ—we can demonstrate his love clearly, tangibly, and boldly.

Read 2 Corinthians 2:14

Lord, teach us to remember that we can do more together than we can apart.

Two-sided Coin

Than to be the king of a vast domain and be held in sin's dread sway.
I'd rather have Jesus than anything this world affords today.

I'D RATHER HAVE JESUS by Rhea F. Miller

Some folks think that Christians have to choose between possessing wealth and influence and having Jesus. Is God more pleased with those on one end of the affluence spectrum than with those on the other? The answer to that lies in the answer to these vital questions: What is our heart's desire? Who or what rules us?

Do we pursue possessions in order to try and fill an empty space inside? Do we use money, power, and property as tools to further God's work and kingdom? Are we generous in sharing our blessings with others?

Do our belongings serve us as we serve God? It's good to take personal inventory on this subject.

Where do we invest the bulk of our assets—our time, money, and energy? Regardless of the amount—small or great—how do we employ more of what we've been given? Allow the generosity of our great God to be seen through you.

Read Joshua 24:15
Align my blessings with Your priorities,
O God.

He Is Alive!

Hallelujah, our Savior is alive! Hallelujah, He is alive!
Jesus Went to the Garden by Marc Byrd and Steve Hindalong

When His followers took Jesus down from the cross, they held His lifeless body in their arms. His lungs had stopped taking breath; His heart had ceased beating.

Strangely, we must fully accept the fact that He died in order to fully embrace His resurrection. We tend to focus on the events prior to His death, probably because it's painful to contemplate the unjust abuse of the Son of God. Yet the truth is, He was dead for three days, not just unconscious for a few hours. His body was cold. Wrapped in grave clothes. Sealed behind a rolling stone in a tomb.

But then on that third day, when He returned to life, His body was so renewed that His followers didn't immediately recognize Him. Once they knew the truth, the good news could not be stopped.

Our Savior lives! Tell the world!

Read John 20:10–18
Jesus, may others see You living in and through me.

Persist

Sometimes I feel discouraged, and think my work's in vain,
but then the Holy Spirit revives my soul again.
THERE IS A BALM IN GILEAD, an African-American spiritual

In the Bible, Gilead was known as a center of healing—a place where the sick could find doctors and medicines in ready supply. Sometimes we become so burdened and weary from ongoing ministry efforts that we require supernatural restoration. The Holy Spirit is our Comforter and Healer who loves us back to strength, allowing us to press on.

By laboring for Christ, we are subject to ridicule and persecution. Our presentation of salvation might fall on deaf ears or be ignored. Our service might be taken for granted or our way forward repeatedly sabotaged, detoured, or blocked.

But hold steady. Don't give in to despair. Press on. God treasures you and everything you do for His glory. Scripture tells us that while we may not actually see fruit from the seeds we sow, He will take care of the increase. Nothing that's done in His name and according to His will is unnecessary, useless, or unproductive.

Read Luke 12:6–7
Holy Spirit, give me the strength to continue that You may be glorified.

A Friend, Indeed

*Jesus knows all about our struggles; He will guide till the day is done;
there's not a friend like the lowly Jesus.*

No, Not One! by Johnson Oatman, Jr.

Now officially a single mother—divorced and alone—Stephanie felt isolated, overwhelmed. What's worse, she was consumed by regret. People had warned her that marrying the man would be a mistake. But at the time, she was in love and sure he had changed; she refused to believe that he would ever go back to his old ways.

We all go through "valley experiences"—trials and struggles that no one but God can help us through, heartaches and heartbreaks that only He can heal. Friends and loved ones may offer occasional comfort, but there will be plenty of times when we find ourselves alone and trembling under the weight of our sorrows.

How wonderful to know that Jesus knows all about our valleys, and He is there to guide us through! There is no friend like Jesus. Look to Him when your heart is breaking.

Read Proverbs 18:24
Lord, thank You for being my Friend.

Eternal Friend

Have we trials and temptations? Is there trouble anywhere?
We should never be discouraged; take it to the Lord in prayer.
WHAT A FRIEND WE HAVE IN JESUS by Joseph M. Scriven

Jesus is both author and finisher of our faith. He gives us the wisdom we lack, reverses discouragement, walks us through trials, and provides the way out of temptations.

As believers, we don't have to labor alone. Christ is able to ease our burdens, light the way, and neutralize enemy attacks. Yet we often try doing everything else before finally resigning ourselves to the fact that there is nothing left to do but pray. In fact, the most potent item in our spiritual arsenal is frequent and fervent prayer, grounded in faith. By putting on the full armor of God during days of spiritual battle, we are able to stand our ground and praise Him, not for our difficulties but in spite of them. Jesus is our eternal Friend and personal Redeemer.

Remember where you were when you first met your Savior? He did not bring you out of Egypt to abandon you now! Seek Him first, regardless of what you face.

Read Philippians 4:6
Lord Most Holy, I praise You. Humbly I submit my circumstances into Your care.

To Whom Much Is Given

Then we shall be where we would be. Then we shall be what we should be.
Praise the Savior by Thomas Kelly

Theodore Kaczynski had every reason to be highly successful, at least on paper. Graduating from high school at the age of fifteen, he scored near the top of his class at Harvard before graduating at age twenty. After earning a PhD in mathematics at the University of Michigan, he was hired as the youngest professor ever to teach at UC Berkeley. How sad and ironic that he subsequently resigned, moved into the wilderness, began a campaign of terrorism, and now lives behind bars, known best as "the Unabomber."

Every person has a unique set of God-given gifts. Few people understand the true value of their talents; some fail to even recognize they have them at all. Lacking purpose, they stray from God's intentions. But God has blessed us in order that we might be a blessing to others.

What is your divine purpose?

Read Ephesians 1:12
Let my talents bring You glory rather than disgrace, dear God.

None like Jehovah

Holy are you, Lord God Almighty.

Agnus Dei by Michael W. Smith

In Isaiah 45, we read about the rare might of our heavenly Father. He declares that there is no other Lord and no other God beside Him.

Study God's names for a beautiful witness of His character of power, everlasting love, and mercy. Jehovah-Jireh: The Lord will provide. Jehovah-Mekaddishkem: The Lord, our sanctifier. Jehovah-Rapha: The Lord who heals. Jehovah-Roi: The Lord, my shepherd. Jehovah-Tsidkenu: The Lord, our righteousness. El-Elyon: Most high God (which emphasizes God as the exalted, sovereign one). El-Olam: Everlasting God. El-Roi: The God who sees. El-Shaddai: God Almighty.

He is holy, Alpha and Omega, the beginning and the end. There is no god like Jehovah! Nothing is outside the province of His power—not time, distance, nature, or any created thing. Praise Him who not only has authority over the setting sun but intimately knows each of His children.

Read Revelation 5:11–14

Holy One of Israel, who was, and is, and is to come...I worship You.

Storm Shelter

Other refuge have I none, hangs my helpless soul on Thee;
leave O leave me not alone, still support and comfort me.

JESUS, LOVER OF MY SOUL by Charles Wesley

Years ago the movie *Twister* told the story of a group of meteorologists chasing tornadoes across the heartland of America. Ravaging storms would devour everything in their path—skipping across the sky, throwing debris in all directions. In one scene, the unpredictable tornado changed direction and overpowered the team. Yet miraculously, in the midst of the raging wind, there came a few moments of calm. The storm chasers were in the eye of the storm.

At times you may feel like a tornado is ravaging your life, leaving nothing but debris in its wake. But of this you can be sure: you don't have to worry about where your protection comes from. Jesus is your refuge—that safe place in the middle of the storm. There is no greater shelter than Him.

Read Isaiah 32:2
Thank You, God, that You are a shelter for my soul!

More than Enough

He gave His life, what more could He give?
O, How He Loves You and Me by Kurt Kaiser

Some people are difficult to please. It seems that no matter what you do, it's not enough for them. The frustration can make you want to give up, move on, and never try again. Yet our God is generous, even to those who ignore or avoid Him. Though people seek to satisfy themselves with the temporary things of this world, Jesus is our treasure— the ultimate Gift. He loved us before we loved Him. He redeemed us and satisfied our every need by giving His life. What more could He possibly have given?

The magnitude of our Savior's love is greater than we can comprehend, but His example is one for us to follow. He not only inspires our giving but motivates it—blessing us far more in our giving than our receiving.

Experience the joy of giving again. Give like God— liberally, sacrificially, and impartially. Pray for others to open their hearts not just to your gift but to the best gift they'll ever receive: salvation.

Read 1 John 3:16
Lord, teach me to give without strings attached.

Fearless

What a fellowship, what a joy divine.... What have I to dread, what have I to fear?
Leaning on the Everlasting Arms by Elisha A. Hoffman

What is your biggest fear? When asked this question, a group of thirty-something adults responded with a variety of answers. Losing a loved one, such as a child or spouse, ranked high on the list for many. Loss of job or career, failure, and terminal illness were also common answers.

If we're willing to admit it, most of us have private worries that distract us or keep us from enjoying peace. As believers, we can let go of our anxiety and cling to our God, who accepts us and promises love, forgiveness, and support. Fellowship with our heavenly Father drives out fear and ushers in peace. There need be no fear or dread because we have assurance of a God who guides, protects, and provides for us...regardless of what comes.

Revel in knowing that God will not leave you. You are safe in His care.

Read Deuteronomy 37:27
I count on the safety I find in Your arms, God.

Reach for the Lifeline

The raging storms may 'round us beat... We'll never leave our safe retreat.
A Shelter in the Time of Storm by Vernon J. Charlesworth

Joseph, Daniel, Ruth, and other biblical ancestors seem like veritable faith giants when we read about the trials they faced and how they responded. Peter, on the other hand, struggled in ways we can easily understand. In the Scriptures, we witness him experiencing fear, anger, doubt, and faith. He was never poker-faced! For instance, in Matthew 14:30 we learn that Peter felt fear and cried out to Jesus to save him as the wind and waves became overwhelming. Most of us can understand how Peter may have felt. After all, we are likely leaving a storm, in the midst of one, or— whether we see it coming or not—about to enter one.

Are you treading water—or maybe even sinking—in an area of your life because you haven't cried out, "Lord, save me"? Don't wait any longer. Stretch out your hand; Someone infinitely trustworthy is waiting. Jesus is a secure lifeline, a safe retreat in the midst of storms (Matthew 14:31).

Read 1 Samuel 2:2
Lord, enable me to keep tight hold of Your hand.

No Cash, No Credit

Let the poor man say I am rich in Him.
LET THE RIVER FLOW by Darrell Paton Evans

Unlike some religious leaders of His time, Jesus preached to the poor and rich alike. He freely offered physical, emotional, and spiritual healing without prejudice, because He saw every person as God's handiwork.

The economic conditions of the past few years have caused people from every walk of life to lose jobs, homes, even their hope. Stories of financial woes abound from Wall Street to Main Street. But one thing remains clear: it is not in money or possessions that we find peace or salvation.

Salvation is a gift that God gives. Everlasting life cannot be earned or purchased; it is freely offered. There is no bribing, buying, or cajoling God's heart for sharing His eternal domain. A simple prayer of faith provides access to His eternal dwelling for rich and poor alike.

Limited financial resources do not diminish spiritual riches. We are rich in ways the world doesn't understand or appreciate. We have an inheritance stored up in heaven that money can't buy and time can't devalue.

Read Ezekiel 47:5–9
Lord, thank You that the poor and rich share equally in Your kingdom.

Bearing Our Crosses

He walked the hill; He bore the cross; this is love.
This Is Love by Terry Butler and Mike Young

Sorrow and anguish are not easy to bear. In those moments when we are weighed down by problems and concerns, and we stagger under the burden of our disappointments, it helps to remember the passion of our Christ. He understands our pain.

Jesus carried the cross on which He was to suffer and die. He did this because He loved us. The Son of God had stepped down from His throne to suffer the worst so that you and I wouldn't have to. The Roman punishment of crucifixion was hallmarked by the degradation of compelling the criminal to carry the very cross upon which he would later be nailed. Jesus was no criminal. He bore the cross not for His crimes but to save the lives of sinners around Him, as well as those yet to be born. On the cross, Jesus endured our punishment.

How do you respond to Jesus's sacrifice of love?

Read John 19:17
Lord Jesus, thank You for dying in my place.

Safe Harbor

The tempest may sweep o'er the wild, stormy deep, in Jesus I'm safe evermore.
The Haven of Rest by H. L. Gilmour

Hurricanes are devastating. Driving, powerful winds cause damage to property and injury to living things. In the same way, the conflict and commotion of life can be frightening and even damage one's faith.

In Mark 4:35–41 our Lord was sleeping during a furious storm. The disciples awakened Him, asking if He cared that they were all about to perish. Jesus calmly responded, saying, "Peace, be still," to the skies. The wind immediately ceased, the sea calmed, and He asked His disciples, "Why are you so fearful?"

What's causing your worry today? Why are you anxious? The events of life can be overwhelming, but to be in Christ is to be safe. There is refuge and guidance in His Word. Protection in His arms as He cares for us. And eternal security through His victory over death.

Christ is forever our haven, our rest. When He speaks, all heaven and earth must obey.

Read Exodus 33:22
Lord, I choose to trust and rest in You, knowing Your hands hold tomorrow.

Making the Bible Your Own

More about Jesus in His Word, holding communion with my Lord,
hearing His voice in every line, making each faithful saying mine.
MORE ABOUT JESUS by Eliza E. Hewitt

When the elderly woman died, some of her friends looked through her Bible and found numerous underlined passages, many marked with stars. Some of the heavily underlined passages were marked with two or even three stars. The woman had quite evidently spent many hours reading God's Word, making each faithful statement her own.

One of the best ways to learn more about Jesus is through reading the Bible. Some people read the Word as if it were any other book, never stopping to consider its deeper meanings. Others study the Bible but get caught up in facts—missing out on the personal application side of it. To learn more about Jesus from His Word, we must read and study it, praying for God's direction and personal conviction as we do.

Spend time meditating on His Word so that its faithful sayings will become the vocabulary of your heart.

Read Psalm 1:1–3
Lord, thank You for Your Word that helps
me know You better.

Soul Sanctuary

Be not dismayed whate'er betide.... No matter what may be the test, God will take care of you.
GOD WILL TAKE CARE OF YOU by Civilla D. Martin

Nothing compares to God's personal assurances. In the beginning of Isaiah 46, God tells us that He will be with us throughout all of life's stages.

This means that no matter what we face, we need not succumb to soul-numbing fears, for we are not on this journey alone. Critical illness, dire financial concerns, or death of loved ones may try our resolve and test our faith. But the presence of God is keenly felt when we determine to keep our eyes on Him and not on situations that threaten to weaken us.

At such times, the promises of Scripture can help to soothe our souls and provide solace. The Word of God reminds us that He not only goes before us, but that in His great love, He provided us with a Comforter. Although some nights may be long, God has given His promise that joy will come with the morning.

Read Isaiah 46:3–4
Father God, thank You for love that gives me strength to not give up.

Constant Companion

Not death, nor life, nor anything, can ever separate me.
His Forever by Pat Sczebel

No matter what we walk through, God is with us. Nothing can separate us from His presence. He holds our hand through unexpected doubt and fear. He strokes our head when we are wretchedly ill. When we are lost in unfamiliar, uncharted territory, He guides us. He comes near when we feel lonely. He puts His arms around us as we grieve the loss of a loved one. He dances with us when good news is delivered. He smiles proudly when we accomplish our goals. He runs with us when we feel strong and energetic. When there is a brilliant sunset, together we embrace the awesome beauty of His creation. He lets us whisper our concerns to Him in the darkness of night when everyone else is asleep.

He is our constant Companion...the one who will never leave us no matter what. Nothing can ever separate us.

Read Psalm 23:4
Lord, thank You for being my constant Companion.

Preferential Treatment

Faithfulness, faithfulness is what You want from me.
TAKE MY LIFE by Scott Underwood

The dictionary defines the word devoted as "dedicated, loyal, committed." These are words we rarely hear anymore, for our world increasingly encourages us to please ourselves and make sure we have "me" time.

Our heavenly Father, however, asks us for something permanent—faithfulness. Regardless of its convenience, He calls us to honor both Him and others above ourselves. Being faithful and true almost always signifies sacrifice, and often means forfeiting our own agenda. But isn't it remarkable to witness the dedication of a godly husband, the surrender of a missionary, the love of a mother?

Devotion is more than the few minutes it takes to read this book each day. "To devote" is a verb; it requires action. We live out our allegiance to the Savior by living out our devotion. By regularly putting aside our own agenda and being faithful to God's will. Thankfully, Jesus modeled this for us and stands ready to help us when we call.

Read Romans 12:10
Help me be so devoted to You, Lord, that I love sacrificially.

Sufficient Grace

The depths of Your grace who can measure? You fully supply all I need.
THE LORD IS by Pat Sczebel and Bob Kauflin

A young couple longed to start a family, but chronic health challenges culminated in the dreaded diagnosis of infertility. While they wanted to trust God to see them through, their hearts were hurting and heavy. One woman in their church suggested they pray Hannah's prayer from 1 Samuel, proclaiming their belief in God's ability to fulfill their heart's desire despite their circumstances. In the end, they were blessed with a beautiful child whom they appropriately named Karis, which in Greek means "grace."

What an unexpected gift Karis was to her parents! Even today, they find it difficult to articulate the full impact of this blessing in their lives, though they try their best to explain it.

God's grace toward us has a similar effect. We know that without it, we would be far different people—heavy-hearted and oppressed, struggling with sin and selfishness, searching for purpose. Because of grace, however, we are redeemed; we are sustained; we are fulfilled. How amazing!

Read Ephesians 1:3
Your grace, Lord, leaves me speechless.

Lighten Your Load

Cast your care on Jesus today, leave your worry and fear.
BURDENS ARE LIFTED AT CALVARY by John M. Moore

Hiking is a grueling sport—backpacks get heavy; bodies grow fatigued and weary. No hiker wants to carry more than necessary. That's why they learn early on how to pack carefully. The challenge is to consider what is needed for the journey and then pare it all down even further, until one has only the absolute essentials.

Life can sometimes feel like an exhausting hike through rugged territory. Many of us are carrying heavy loads that wear us down and weaken our resolve. However, as believers it's not necessary to bear the weight ourselves. Jesus is near; we can cast our cares on Him.

On Calvary He paid the price. On Calvary He relieved us of our burdens and offered rest for our weary souls. Calvary covers all our cares. Let Jesus handle your load.

Read Romans 5:6
Help us to cast all our cares on You, Jesus.

Shouldering the Weight

My guilt and despair Jesus took on Him there, and Calvary covers it all.
CALVARY COVERS IT ALL by Mrs. Walter G. Taylor

Have you ever carried a heavy box and needed an extra hand to reach for a door handle? Or maybe you put the package down and opened the swinging door but couldn't keep it open long enough to make it inside? You needed someone to open the door or carry the load.

The miracle of Calvary is that Jesus did for us that which we couldn't do for ourselves. He lifted the cumbersome load of guilt we carried. He released us from the awkward heap of despair over what we couldn't fix.

And He opened the door and held it—giving us access to a place where we'll never have to pick up those loads again.

Is there a wearisome weight you're still struggling to bear, something you think is too shameful to let Jesus shoulder? His focus is your freedom, and He can handle anything you are ready to release.

Read Colossians 2:13
Please remove this heavy burden, God, and lead me to freedom in You.

Divine Sustainer

Bread of Life, You are Sustainer.
So Good by Jennie Riddle

To be sustained means to be nurtured, protected, and kept. That is exactly what God does for us.

The biblical name Jehovah-Jireh recognizes God as our principal provider. He can satisfy our every need—emotional, financial, or spiritual. Jehovah-Shalom tells us He is our God of peace. Wars and economic difficulties add to the daily stresses and threaten our internal peace, but God provides a calm that goes beyond circumstances.

Though He never promised us we would be free from difficult situations, He did promise that He would never leave us nor forsake us. In this age where independence and self-sufficiency are heralded as virtues, we must never lose sight of the fact that when we rely on God as our sustainer, we can press on in faith.

Read Psalm 55:22
God, I don't know what I would do without Your promise to uphold me in every way.

Jesus, Our Prize

Jesus, our only joy be Thou, as Thou our prize wilt be.
Jesus, be Thou our glory now and through eternity.
JESUS, THE VERY THOUGHT OF THEE, attributed to Bernard of Clairvaux

Winning feels great. The recognition that comes with a first-place trophy, gold medal, or blue ribbon is rewarding. Yet reality sets in when we remember that next year, someone else will likely be crowned number one.

As believers, we can delight that while our ranking here on earth is temporary, we have a great eternal reward in Jesus. Whether we're first or last, our consolation lies in understanding that our joy is in our salvation—our joy is in Jesus, our Savior. Comfort and rest from life's rat race await us in the blessed assurance of His ongoing presence in our lives. Come what may, we can rejoice in knowing that Jesus is always there caring, guiding, and directing us.

Our hope is misplaced in our own abilities, and the pursuit of earthly riches is futile and foolish. The one, true goal—the only one that guarantees us placement in the winners' circle—is to grow closer to Him daily by humbly submitting to His will in our lives.

Read Hebrews 12:3
Lord Jesus, draw me closer so that I may rely on You and You alone.

Wake Up in Winning Mode

When you wake up in the morning, Jesus gonna pull you through.
Jesus Is the Rock, and He Rolls My Blues Away by Tony Congi

Think about this. The very fact that you got out of bed this morning is evidence that you are in it to win it. Why else would God have awakened you? Do you think He would watch over you while you slept and protect you from harm all these years for you to be defeated? Not a chance.

You have everything you need to be a living testimony to God's strength. Not just a new day but new mercies for the journey.

God's love for you is so great that you cannot be overcome by your circumstances. You can endure and triumph over today's challenges, assured that He is with you and ready to use you.

The fact that you woke up this morning is all the proof you need.

Read Lamentations 3:22–23
Lord, make me an overcomer today.

Say What?

Take joy, my King, in what You hear.

I Love You, Lord by Laurie Klein

God is a silent witness to every conversation we have. He hears every word, whether spoken in jest, anger, love, or greed. He hears words that uplift our family and friends, and those that do not. He hears words that bless, and words that curse.

His own ways with His children teach us about His intentions for us. God does not verbally abuse us. He speaks lovingly to us, realizing we are weak. He speaks with us, not to us. He never talks down to us or treats us according to our worst behavior. Even in His correction, our heavenly Father builds us up.

Reading the Bible gives us a clear picture of the power of words as well. Psalms cheer us, Proverbs give us wisdom, Romans points to repentance, Philippians exhorts, and Jude gently rebukes.

What books or verses of the Bible speak most to you? What do they reveal about the way God wants you to speak to others?

Read Ephesians 4:29
Lord, help me express myself in words that bless You and others.

Deep Love

It was my sin that held Him there until it was accomplished.
How Deep the Father's Love for Us by Stuart Townend

While running through the house, a toddler fell and got a deep cut on his head. His mother raced him to the emergency room. There, the doctor instructed her to hold her son still while he stitched the boy's forehead. Holding the child still through the process was agony for the mother; the boy couldn't understand why his mom was letting the doctor do this! But she knew that he had to endure the pain in order to heal. Until his wound was sewn back together, she wasn't letting go.

God allowed His Son to suffer so that our relationship with Him might be healed. It was the only way to bring restoration in our relationship with Him. Sometimes God allows us to suffer too, knowing it is the only way we will grow and blossom down the road.

In the moment, our suffering doesn't seem fair or loving. But we can trust our Father's love—always.

Read 1 John 4:9–10
Dear God, thank You for loving me even when I don't realize it. Help me to remember the next time I am hurting.

Sacrificial Giving

God sent not his Son into the world to condemn the world,
but that the world through him might be saved.
God So Loved the World by John Stainer

Sickness and death plagued a community in India because the people were forced to drink dirty water. A church in America heard of their plight and sent a love offering to missionaries who planned to build a well to provide the people with clean water. But once the church sent off that first check, they didn't stop there. They realized there were other communities that needed clean water too, so that body of believers continued to send the resources necessary to build other wells.

Our God knew that all of humankind was condemned by sin, so He made a way for us to be freed from its bondage. In His great love, He provided a solution—a well full of clean water for a sick and dying people: Jesus.

Read John 3:16–17
Your healing, sacrificial love truly makes a difference in my life, Lord.

A Royal Pen Pal

O the pure delight of a single hour that before Thy throne I spend;
when I kneel in prayer and with Thee, my God, I commune as friend with friend.

I Am Thine, O Lord by Fanny J. Crosby

For fourteen years, an ordinary tram driver in Russia had been a pen pal with the queen of England. When he first wrote to her in 1997, he never expected a reply, but he has since received more than twenty letters from her. He continues to write to her on special occasions.

Although we may not realize it, we too have the opportunity to communicate with royalty. The King of kings has invited us into communion with Him, but we don't have to wait to receive a reply by letter. He is as close as a simple prayer, and He loves to hear from us. Our King is not a distant monarch but one who loves us and who—through His death—has made us His friends.

Think of it, we have the ear of the King! What a privilege it is to spend time communicating with Him, our Friend.

Read Exodus 33:11
Thank You, my King, for the opportunity to talk with You.

Author of Eternity

We blossom and flourish as leaves on the tree,
and wither and perish—but naught changeth Thee.
Immortal, Invisible by Walter Chalmers Smith

Have you ever noticed the complexity of a pinecone or the delicate petals of a daffodil? They are radically different plants, yet each has its own role and its own brand of beauty. The pine tree grows tall and strong, lasting for decades, if not centuries. The blossoms of a daffodil burst out for only a short time yet return each year.

The Creator of both pine and flower is the eternal One. He is the same yesterday, today, and forever. Nothing changes Him. His promises and purposes are forever true, forever the same.

We are more like the seeds of the many plants on this planet; God created each of us with different looks, roles, purposes. We blossom and flourish for a specific time frame on this earth, and then we are gone. We too "wither and perish."

So bloom today. Let God's beauty and purpose shine through you, whether you have decades or days left here on earth.

Read Hebrews 13:8
Thank You, God, for Your eternal character.

Thou Art Holy

*Though the eye of sinful man Thy glory may not see, only Thou art holy;
there is none beside Thee—perfect in power, in love and purity.*

Holy, Holy, Holy! Lord God Almighty! by Reginald Heber

Sometimes the God of the Old Testament seems different from the God of the New Testament. It's as if He was once a God of anger, wrath, and jealousy, but now He is a Comforter—bringing love, joy, and peace. The contrast can seem strong enough for us to question which God we should believe in. This perceived disparity is a human misconception.

God is holy and just—as He always has been. Because of this, in the days of the Old Testament He gave His people specific instructions regarding sacrifice for their sin.

Likewise, the New Testament tells us how, in His holiness, He provided the perfect sacrifice—His Son, Jesus—in order that sinful man would have access to an almighty Redeemer. He is worthy of our grateful honor and praise for making a way to overcome the grip of sin.

Only our King could use His power for such pure and loving purposes.

Read Revelation 4:8
You are always holy, God. How great You are!

Worthy

No one more worthy of songs to be sung.

JOYOUS LIGHT, author unknown, arrangement by Chris Tomlin, David Crowder, and Louis Giglio

We make celebrities out of the people we most admire. For instance, the Super Bowl showcases our best in football every year. Commentators gather to discuss and praise individual players, while fans purchase expensive game tickets and wear their favorite players' jerseys. These athletes and everything associated with them become the center of attention in our nation. In fact, every sport, every music genre, and the movie industry all host an "ultimate" celebration of their "best"—those who are worthy of special recognition.

But there is One who deserves our praise more than any of these, One who is far more admirable than any athlete, musician, or actor: Jesus. Let us lift Him up to be glorified rather than any human achiever. Who could be more worthy of our honor and praise than the Savior of the world?

Read 1 Chronicles 16:23–26
I give You my highest praise today, Lord.

All People Everywhere

'Til ev'ry tribe and tongue voices Your praise, send us out.
MISSION'S FLAME by Matt Redman

In a vision of heaven, John saw a crowd of people standing before God's throne. Clothed in brilliant white garments and shouting praises to Jesus and His Father, these ransomed, faithful believers were, John perceived, representatives of literally every race on earth.

While celebrating diversity is a fairly recent phenomenon in our culture, it has been God's plan for populating heaven all along. Yet how will they believe unless they hear, the apostle Paul asked rhetorically, and how will they hear unless someone goes (Romans 10:13–15)? This doesn't mean we all must head to the far reaches of the world; even neighbors on your block might not have heard the Word. But we must go where He sends us. Jesus told His disciples, "The harvest truly is plentiful, but the laborers are few. Therefore pray the Lord of the harvest to send out laborers into His harvest" (Matthew 9:37–38 NKJV).

Could you be one of them?

Read Revelation 7:9–17
I'm willing to go. Lord, send me.

Draw Near

He owns me for His child; I can no longer fear.
With confidence I now draw nigh, and "Father, Abba, Father," cry.

ARISE, MY SOUL, ARISE by Charles Wesley

Most children adore their fathers—they look up to them, long to have time with them, and instinctively know that when Daddy is around, they are safe.

God understands our desire for a strong and loving refuge, and as our heavenly Father He meets that need. Like any good father, He loves us, His children, more than anything in the world. He longs for a relationship with us—that we would adore Him, look to Him for help and guidance, seek time with Him, and know that when He is with us, we are safe.

We need not be afraid. We are children of our Father, the King. But His name is also "Abba"—literally, "Daddy." He loves us so much He sent His Son to save us. We can draw close to Him; we are a part of His divine family.

Draw near with confidence. Your Father loves you.

Read Hebrews 4:16

Thank You, God, for letting me confidently draw close to You.

The Firm Foundation

Your love is amazing, steady and unchanging.
HALLELUJAH by Brenton Brown and Brian Doerksen

Years ago a thirteen-story building collapsed in Shanghai, China. The apartment complex was under construction. It was supposed to give homes to five hundred people, but it ended up taking a person's life. According to Chinese newspapers, the building collapsed due to improper planning and failure to stabilize the structure's foundation.

The basics are important. Without a firm foundation, even a beautifully designed building will come crashing to the ground. In a similar way, if God is not the cornerstone of our lives, we condemn ourselves to ruin, regardless of what heights our plans help us reach. We need the firm foundation God provides to live a stable life. Therefore, as we build our lives on His promises, He will support us in all we do. God is strong, steadfast, and unchanging. We can rely on Him to withstand every force that comes our way.

Read Matthew 7:24–27
You are our firm foundation, Lord. Help me to build on You and You alone.

Ambassadors of Christ

All these things shall be added unto you.
Seek Ye First by Karen Lafferty

An ambassador's sole purpose is to serve his nation. Ambassadors promote national concerns, not individual ideologies. Only one agenda item rules the day: represent the nation well, at all times.

Our priorities—the things we do first—should reflect our status as ambassadors of Christ. We represent the kingdom of God. We should conduct kingdom affairs with excellence. As spokespersons of the King of kings and the Lord of lords, our purpose is to promote the Good News of Christ's life, death, resurrection, and return.

Living like an ambassador of Christ will allow you to prioritize your day. Choosing between the good idea and the God idea—between the eternal focus and the earthly focus—becomes easier when you know to seek His kingdom first.

Worrying about daily needs is futile; our King has already made provision. You are an ambassador of Christ and you have everything you need to represent Him well.

Read Matthew 6:33
God, show me how to live like the kingdom of God is at hand.

Prayer Posture

Draw me to my knees so we can talk.
Oh, Lead Me by Martin Smith

In our modern sophisticated era, few still get on their knees to pray. Yet through the centuries, generations of God's people have thought of this as the most natural posture in which to place themselves before God. When we get down on our knees, we recognize our humble position and dependence on the heavenly Father.

After all, we don't have to exalt ourselves. He has already done that by claiming us as sons and daughters, promising heavenly citizenship, and providing personal fellowship. Through Jesus Christ, we can come boldly into the very throne room of God and speak with Him face to face. Many of us find that on our knees, we more easily sense that ready access; we relax and loosen up, and sweet conversation with our Lord ensues.

Try it. But be careful. Once you start talking with Him, you may not get up for a while.

Read Daniel 6:10
Lord, I'm down on my knees. Let's talk, just You and me.

Down for the Count

Love's redeeming work is done, alleluia! Fought the fight, the battle won, alleluia!
CHRIST THE LORD IS RISEN TODAY by Charles Wesley

Professional heavyweight boxing matches tend to go twelve rounds max. Throughout the three-minute sets, each athlete wars against the other in hopes of receiving the championship title. When the fight is through, the opponents are battered, yet one leaves the ring victorious.

God loves His creation and He does not want to be separated from us. However, our sin nature is a formidable opponent and our enemy relentlessly stalks us. Because of His great passion for us, God sent Jesus to be our substitute in a match we could not win.

Jesus was battered and bruised and died for our sins; but thankfully, He did not lose the fight—the grave could not hold down the Son of God. He rose in triumph! God's love provided a way for all humankind to have the final victory over sin.

Whose side of the ring are you on?

Read Mark 16:6
I praise You, Lord, for being the reigning victor!

Feeling God's Presence

I can feel His mighty power and His grace.
SURELY THE PRESENCE OF THE LORD by Lanny Wolfe

After the loss of both her father and sister within two weeks of each other, a longtime Christian expressed her gratitude for the many prayers lifted up on her behalf. She went on to share that it was only her heavenly Father that was helping her hold it together. She admitted she was focused on little more than Him; leaning on her Lord helped her get through each day. As a result, she testified that she could tangibly feel His presence with her as she moved through each hour.

It's incredible to know that we have a personal God who loves us dearly and longs to share in our lives. If we want to feel His tangible presence in our lives, oftentimes we must simply turn down the noise and turn toward Him.

Read Acts 2:1–2
Lord, thank You for the opportunity to turn to You and know You're present in everything I see, hear, and do throughout the day.

Trusting God to Lead

Nothing will I fear as long as You are near.
Thy Word by Michael W. Smith and Amy Grant

The enemy of our souls wishes to lead us into darkness and danger. He aspires to cloud our lives with uncertainty and fear. He knows we will stumble and fall in such obscurity and lose sight of God's path.

Thankfully, though, Jesus is our light. His Word is a lamp for our feet, lighting up our path so that we can move forward, one step at a time. It is vital to the life of the believer to always walk in the Word. In doing so, we can confidently allow God to guide our steps and direct our paths.

When we fool ourselves into relying on our own abilities, we find that we're just making ourselves a bigger target for the enemy, rummaging in the darkness and continuing to stumble. Only God knows what lies ahead. He is, after all, the Creator of the future. We can trust Him to lead our way.

Read Psalm 119:105
Lord, I am trusting in Your Word to lead me through this day.

Our Sufficiency

Jesus, my Shepherd, Brother, Friend, my Prophet, Priest, and King.
How Sweet the Name of Jesus Sounds by John Newton

Jesus plays an integral role in the life of every believer. He is Immanuel—God with us—actively engaged in the lives of His people on earth. For His followers, He guides and provides; He is our Shepherd. He never sleeps nor slumbers; He keeps constant watch over us. He sticks closer than a brother; we can trust and depend on Him. He is the spoken Word and ultimate prophet; He was there at the beginning and already knows the end. It is comforting to know that, as our Creator, He understands us. As our priest, He is sitting at the right hand of the Father, interceding for us. As our King, He rules over every circumstance and fights every battle for us.

Today, He wants you to know just how much He loves you. He wants to shelter, guide, and protect you. Jesus longs to befriend you and spend time with you.

Read 1 Corinthians 1:2
Jesus, You are all I will ever need or want.

Natural Praise

The heavens declare Your greatness; the oceans cry out to You.
MAJESTIC by Lincoln Brewster

Everything praises the Lord. Everything! Cheetahs race across the tundra, eagles soar, and grizzlies fish for salmon. Ocean waves roar, trees sway, flowers bloom, and mountains stand proud. If all of God's creation praises Him just by functioning the way He designed it, then why shouldn't we?

Take a few lessons from nature. Worms and ants, rain and clouds—each one does as God planned, all the while displaying who He is. What about you? Your obedience to God reveals His presence in your life. When you fulfill the purpose He has uniquely designed you for, your life becomes a song of praise.

Read Psalm 19:1
Your praise is continually in my mouth, O Lord.

Unlimited Access

Though millions have come, there's still room for one. There's room at the Cross for you.
THERE'S ROOM AT THE CROSS by Ira F. Stanphill

In just about every restaurant, concert hall, or public place wherever folks come together, you'll find a "maximum occupancy" sign. These are typically posted and enforced by a local fire marshal in order to ensure that people can gather safely without risk of over-crowding. To avoid being overwhelmed by a crowd, many people prefer to go to outdoor events where there's space to freely move about. However, in such a mass of people, one can still feel overwhelmed and insecure.

Thankfully, there are no limitations on the number of people that can come to the cross for spiritual healing. God, through Jesus's sacrifice, makes salvation available to any and all who care to approach. He is always accessible, always present—personally listening to the cries of our hearts and the praises of His people.

Read Romans 5:8
Savior, thank You that I can come to the cross...just as I am.

Yield Signs

No longer will we give our hearts to the things of this world.
For a debt of love we will offer to You.

HOLY IS THE LORD by Jeff Searles

After a painful divorce, a young woman who was questioning her faith eventually strayed from her intimate relationship with Christ. Looking for satisfaction in people, entertainment, and possessions, she longed for contentment and approval. However, the more she searched, the more she discovered the unending cycle of grasping for fulfillment that proved increasingly elusive.

Jesus died so that we could live life more abundantly than that. He promises fulfillment and satisfaction in Him. In exchange, He wants our whole hearts. Surrendering is not something we can do on our own; we need the Spirit to empower and equip us to live a surrendered life.

Once you give your life completely to God, what the world offers grows less and less satisfying. Only in His abiding presence will you find total contentment.

Read Romans 12:1–2

I celebrate being completely sold out to You, God.

Divine Guidance

O Holy Spirit, teach us to listen.
O HOLY SPIRIT by Cory DeAngelo

Have you ever observed a new class of kindergarteners? They've not yet learned the classroom rules, and many are new to the concept of school. In other words, initially the classroom is chaotic. Yet within a few weeks, under the guidance of a disciplined teacher, those young ones discover what it means to exercise self-control.

As followers of Christ, we need that same type of direction and support to make good decisions. Maneuvering through the twists, turns, and hurdles of life can sometimes get us off track and distract us from our service to Him. And that leads to a certain adult-level chaos. However, the Holy Spirit was provided to be our Guide and lead us in the way we should go. By actively seeking His discernment and control, we're able to understand the mind of Christ; this helps us make choices that honor God and help direct others into a right relationship with Him.

Read John 14:26
Holy Spirit, teach me to listen to Your voice.

Coming Again

One day to earth He is coming for me. Then with what joy
His dear face I shall see. O how I praise Him—He's coming for me!
WOUNDED FOR ME by Gladys Westcott Roberts

In today's culture it's common for family members to live across the country, or even the globe, from one another. While phone calls, e-mails, and Skype lessen the distance, nothing takes the place of a personal visit. Once the travel plans are arranged, the exciting countdown to the day of arrival begins. And the reunion that occurs when we finally embrace those we've missed so much is emotional!

Isn't it incredible to think that Jesus is returning just for you? Have you considered what you will do and how you will react when He comes to take you home? Praise God that He loves us so much that He's willing to send Jesus a second time to complete the work He started.

Have you told anyone about the great reunion ahead? All who have believed and joined God's family are invited.

Read Acts 1:11
Gracious God, as we look toward the heavens, we anticipate Your return.

Family Connections

Though sufferings may fill our lives, we're confident we're heirs with Christ.
THE FATHER'S LOVE by Joel Sczebel

When pain or loss strikes one member of a family, it affects the whole clan. We don't begin to doubt our familial bond just because there's misery or grief. As a matter of fact, hardship often strengthens the connection between family members.

It is the same within the family of God. Grief will strike; hardship will come—just as it does to every family. After all, Christ—our brother—suffered, so none of us is exempt. The good news, however, is that He overcame both temptation and the grave. And because we are His kin, we too can claim triumph.

Trials and pain will come. When they do, our brothers and sisters will need us, and we'll need them. Yet there's no reason to lose hope or grow weary in doing well. We are part of a family that will go on forever—a family with God as its protector and head.

Read 2 Corinthians 4:17
Our fellowship with You, Jesus, sustains us through momentary afflictions.

Desperate Praise

We bow down and worship Him now, how great, how awesome is He.
HOLY IS THE LORD by Chris Tomlin

Humility is an honorable character trait—but it's more than just a notion. Bowing down requires us to be prostrate, to become powerless, to let go of our own aspirations. There's no more significant act of humility than to empty yourself and give total allegiance to another. And who is more worthy of devoted worship than our awesome Creator and Savior, the Author and Finisher of our faith? After all, Jesus left His throne—sacrificing all power—for death on the cross.

We honor our God by embracing gratitude for Him who, in His holiness, held mankind responsible for sin and yet also gave us a path to redemption. The very thought is mind-boggling—but that's the way of our God, working in ways that are above and beyond all we might imagine. The Almighty One is capable of awesome grace and power. Praise Him!

Read Psalm 68:32–35

Father, I humbly repent of not always giving You the respect You so rightfully deserve.

Nothing but the Name

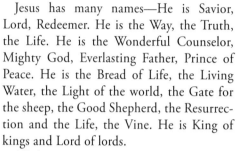

Nothing has the power to save but Your Name.
Your Name by Paul Baloche and Glenn Packiam

Jesus has many names—He is Savior, Lord, Redeemer. He is the Way, the Truth, the Life. He is the Wonderful Counselor, Mighty God, Everlasting Father, Prince of Peace. He is the Bread of Life, the Living Water, the Light of the world, the Gate for the sheep, the Good Shepherd, the Resurrection and the Life, the Vine. He is King of kings and Lord of lords.

All these names point to one thing: He is the only path to salvation. People sometimes object to this belief because, in our society, tolerance of other religions is not just expected, it is demanded. But all religions are not equal. Only Christianity has a God who was willing to die for all of us, providing a permanent sacrifice for our sins.

Only through Jesus Christ can we be saved. Nothing has the power to redeem but His name.

Read John 14:6–7
I call upon Your name, Jesus, and praise You for saving me!

God of the Universe

Ponder anew what the Almighty can do, if with His love He befriend thee.
PRAISE TO THE LORD, THE ALMIGHTY by Joachim Neander

What if you could be friends with the most influential person in your school, at your workplace, or even in the country? You would feel empowered, knowing that you have the ear of the one who can make a difference—someone who will take your thoughts and ideas seriously and keep your best interests in mind.

Now imagine if you were friends with the Ruler of the universe. What if this powerful Friend knew everything that happened in the past and would happen in the future?

Suppose that Friend promised to always give you perfect guidance and vowed to always watch over you?

Well, you do. God reaches out to you and offers His invaluable friendship. Ponder anew what the almighty God can do—He is a Friend like no other.

Read Proverbs 18:24
Lord, for befriending us, we owe You all our gratitude.

Lord of the Hours

Teach me Thy will, and Thy rich promises in me fulfill.... I need Thee, every hour I need Thee.
I NEED THEE EVERY HOUR by Annie S. Hawks

Every day is filled with surprises. As each one starts, we enter into a world filled with the potential for challenge and temptation. The only safe way to proceed is to take Jesus with us. We can rely on Him as we prepare for work, as we get the kids off to school, as we drive in our cars and deal with difficult people or tedious tasks.

We do need Him every hour; we are strengthened when He is near. When we prayerfully walk with Him—allowing Him to show us His will throughout the day (as opposed to our own)—He will fulfill His purposes through us.

Have you invited Jesus to be the Lord of your hours? When you surrender every action and relationship to Him, life will be filled with purpose, peace, joy, and the knowledge that you are precisely where He wants you to be.

Read Matthew 6:8
Father, help me find peace by relying on You.

Father Knows Best

O send Thy Spirit, Lord, now unto me, that He may touch my eyes and make me see.
BREAK THOU THE BREAD OF LIFE by Alexander Groves

The popular 1950s television show *Father Knows Best* portrayed an idealized view of a middle-class American family that is fondly remembered by many who grew up watching the show. For thirty minutes each week, the dad, Jim Anderson, calmly solved his family's problems. Even though the children didn't always agree with their father, in the end they always heeded his advice because they realized that "father knows best."

When life gets difficult, we too must learn to heed the advice of our heavenly Father. God's children have a myriad of problems for which they need advice. The key to solving them is to learn to see them the way He does and to allow our Father—through the Holy Spirit—to revive and renew us as we sort through the challenges.

Read Psalm 19
Precious Father, You always know what is best for me. Remind me of that today.

Proof

Our hearts are hungry for the power of the Lord to be displayed in all the earth.
YOUR GREAT RENOWN by Eric Grover

Do you ever get tired of hearing about Mother Nature as if "she" were responsible for this planet? People often fail to recognize that it was the might of God that spoke the earth—and everything in it—into being.

The wonder of His glory is all around us. One has only to watch the sky turn bright orange as the sun sets over the horizon, enjoy a springtime walk in the Carolinas while flowering trees are in full bloom, or drive along a coastal highway at high tide to observe God's best. His glory is evident in the face of a newborn child peacefully sleeping in his mother's arms, an elderly couple walking hand in hand in the park, or a family brought together by adoption. Yes, God's glory is evident throughout the earth.

Today, take a few moments to stop, examine, and appreciate His many wonders.

Read Isaiah 40:28
Creator God, our world reflects Your glory. Let me proclaim Your glory without hesitation.

America, Bless God

Beautiful Savior! Lord of all the nations! Son of God and Son of Man!
FAIREST LORD JESUS by seventeenth-century German Jesuits

One Sunday morning a pastor preached about the state of the world and the constant barrage of discouraging news from the media. But then, instead of concluding with an end-times message, he did something unusual; he raised a banner that said AMERICA, BLESS GOD.

The congregation immediately stirred, thinking they'd found an error. "Shouldn't the banner read GOD BLESS AMERICA?" someone asked.

"No," he replied. "It's time America begins to bless God."

As believers, we must keep in mind that God is, and always has been, in control despite what's happening in our world. There is no need to worry. He is the Ruler of all nations, including our own.

Read 1 Timothy 6:15–16
I bless You today, God, for our freedom and Your protection. Have mercy on our nation.

Heirs to the Kingdom

Riches I heed not, nor man's empty praise, Thou mine inheritance, now and always.
BE THOU MY VISION by Mary Byrne

Some folks are happy to inherit a business, thinking that it will be their ticket to lifelong security. Others are the beneficiaries of family wealth and prominence. Yet none of these things are guaranteed to last, much less satisfy our souls.

Thankfully, our heavenly inheritance will never go bankrupt or fail. It cannot be lost or stolen or suffer ruin or depreciation. In fact, it only increases in value as our heavenly Father pours out His abundance and grace.

None of us knows what tomorrow may hold for our lives here on earth. Our material wealth, our health, and even our reputations can be lost in an instant. But if we have trusted in Christ, then our inheritance is secure. And no one can ever take that away.

Read Proverbs 3:5
Dear Lord, train my heart to focus on the things that last.

Yes, Jesus Loves Me!

Little ones to Him belong. They are weak, but He is strong....
Yes, Jesus loves me! The Bible tells me so.

JESUS LOVES ME! THIS I KNOW by Anna B. Warner

The lyrics have been taught to children for generations: "Jesus loves me, this I know, for the Bible tells me so..." Such simple words, and yet they reveal so much about Christ's devotion. The gospel message really is as simple as "Yes, Jesus loves me."

When you start to forget this truth, turn to God's Word...and listen. In its pages you'll hear again of God's unconditional love: "Who shall separate us from the love of Christ?" (Romans 8:35 NKJV). "We love Him because He first loved us" (1 John 4:19 NKJV). "For God so loved the world..." (John 3:16 NKJV).

There will be times in life when you will feel unworthy of love, or times when so many negative things happen that you are tempted to believe that God doesn't care. Ask your Lord to help you reject that thinking. Take your thoughts captive and replace them with the truth: "Yes, Jesus loves me."

Read Proverbs 8:17
Gracious Father, when I start to doubt, help me to take my thoughts captive and remember how much You love me.

Dependable

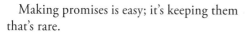

Forever God is faithful; forever God is strong.
FOREVER by Chris Tomlin

Making promises is easy; it's keeping them that's rare.

Most promise makers are well-intentioned. Yet every day, people are hurt because of a promise that wasn't kept. That is why we need a Redeemer—one who cannot and will not change His mind. A constant source of truth and grace. A Savior who can fill the gaps that are left when the going gets too tough or we get distracted or grow weary.

Thankfully, God is always faithful to His promises—regardless of their size. The Bible says it well: His character is holy and good. He is unchanging. What He says lasts forever. He is mighty and true.

With God, forever means eternity; His word is secure. Therefore, everything He has guaranteed to you will come true. Read the Scriptures, go to Him in prayer, and walk by faith.

He will go before you and sustain you with His strength. Forever.

Read Psalm 145:13
Help me to be faithful in the promises I make and to trust You in Yours, God.

Celebrate!

When clothed in His brightness transported I rise to meet Him in clouds of the sky,
His perfect salvation, His wonderful love, I'll shout with the millions on high.

HE HIDETH MY SOUL by Fanny J. Crosby

Part of the anticipation of any big event is in the preparation. We make arrangements to attend a wedding, not just by confirming our reservation for the reception but by buying a gift for the couple and choosing what we will wear.

Can you imagine the preparations that are going on in heaven as Jesus plans for you to join Him at His wedding feast? Are you ready for that momentous occasion? Have you RSVP'd to your invitation? Have you put on the robes of righteousness that have been tailor-made for you?

Praise God that your place at the table is being held; He has taken care of all the arrangements.

Read Exodus 33:22
Thank You, God, for preparing a place for me.

Life through Death

The wonderful cross bids me come and die and find that I may truly live.
THE WONDERFUL CROSS by Jesse Reeves and Chris Tomlin

When you were a kid, did your teacher have you plant a seed in a cup so you could watch it grow? What you probably didn't realize was that the seed you started with had to die to produce the plant that eventually grew in its place.

Just like that seed, we are capable of growth and new life. Lovely blossoms and vibrant fruit are possible. But we must die to our selfish desires first. Christ sacrificed His own life to make abundant life possible for us. Only when we give up ourselves and take on the life of Christ do we become mature in Him.

The world says otherwise, but we'll never change our quality of life in our own strength. We can't find peace or experience healing in a bottle, through a relationship, or on a vacation. We can only obtain life abundant when we understand and live out the way of the cross. Otherwise, we merely exist.

Read Isaiah 53:4
Lord, thank You for dying so that I might fully live.

Victory Is Won

Proclaiming peace, announcing news of happiness.
OUR GOD REIGNS by Leonard E. Smith, Jr.

One of the most famous photos in US history was taken on August 14, 1945. The photo, entitled *V-J Day in Times Square*, captured a young sailor—just back from war—kissing a nurse in a moment of elation. In the background, you can see that the area is filled with sailors and civilians—all celebrating Japan's surrender and an end to World War II.

In those rare times when a nation gains victory over its enemy, celebrations spontaneously break out. But as followers of Christ, we don't have to wait for such landmark occasions. Joy is ours every day because God has been victorious over all things—including sin and death.

It's a new day in the Lord. Spread the word...and celebrate!

Read Isaiah 52:7
Victory is Yours, Lord. The battle has already been won.

Ministering Spirits

And I know that there are angels all around.
HOLY GROUND by Geron Davis

Louis was home by himself, working on a project in his basement, when a spark caught his shirt on fire. Suddenly the flames surrounded him. He tried rolling on the ground, but the fire continued to burn. In that desperate moment, he called out to God and suddenly the fire died out.

Suppose God used angels to spare Louis's life? Perhaps He sent them to douse the flames. Hebrews 1:14 tells us that angels are ministering spirits. They are the extension of God on earth, assisting His followers in their time of need. They are attentive to the prayers we utter and stand ready to help us at God's command. So there's no need to worry; God has placed angels all around you to keep you and protect you—on call at a moment's notice.

Read Psalm 56:7
You have placed your angels all around me.
Your care for me is a blessing.

When Morning Dawns

We follow not with fears, for gladness breaks like morning where'er thy face appears.
Lead On, O King Eternal by Ernest W. Shurtleff

Do you remember what it meant to you to see the sun shining again after a severe storm had passed? Do you remember how it felt to see the light of day dawning after a fearful night?

Suddenly you could believe again that all would be well.

Light does that. It restores our faith, lifts our spirits, gives us a fresh burst of hope where there was none before. Nothing dispels the darkness so quickly. Nothing draws us so instantly out of our defeat and despair.

It is no coincidence, then, that Jesus called Himself the Light of the world. Restorer, Lifter, Dispeller—He is all these and more. Because of Him, fear does not have the last word; the darkness does not win. So go ahead, lift your head. Your Joy has come.

Read 2 Corinthians 4:7–9
Lord, You are my light and salvation. Whom shall I fear?

Beyond a Reasonable Doubt

I need no other argument, I need no other plea;
it is enough that Jesus died and that He died for me.
My Faith Has Found a Resting Place by Lidie H. Edmunds

In a court of law, the strongest cases are backed by physical evidence, a motive, and eyewitness accounts. And even then, if there is a reasonable doubt, the case might be dismissed.

In the "case" for Jesus, there is plenty of support. He physically walked this earth— even objective historians of His day report this as fact. God had a clear motive for sending Him to earth—to bring us back into a relationship with Him. Thousands of people witnessed His works and His integrity, all of which laid further claim to His identity as the Son of God. But still, despite the preponderance of evidence, humanity doubts Him, and debates about Him persist.

The truth is, we were born sinful. Jesus died and rose for each of us. These are facts we can rest in. We need no other argument, no other evidence.

Read Luke 23:46
Jesus, You have proved yourself to me. Guard me from unbelief.

A Church Called Home

I've found where I belong, I'm a living stone, and in this house I will grow.
AWESOME IN THIS PLACE by Ned Davies

Roll into a new town or city, and within a few blocks you're bound to find a church. They're everywhere, each offering programs, fellowship, and worship opportunities, but all geared to helping children and adults grow in the knowledge of Christ Jesus.

Some churches are strictly denominational, others are independent. There are those that boast traditional structures, while others utilize old storefronts, converted theaters, or sports arenas. Some are tiny, others are huge.

There is no "one size fits all" church. Whether you're seeking your first church or a new one due to a life transition, choose one you can call "home." Look for a place where you can plant yourself and grow through fellowship, worship, and solid teaching. Prayerfully, you'll discover a dynamic body of believers with whom you can grow, serve, and connect.

And if you already love your church home, consider sharing it with family and friends who may be searching.

Read 1 Peter 2:5
Lord, lead me to invest in a church where I can grow up spiritually.

So Sing!

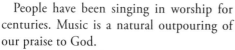

Then let our songs abound and every tear be dry.
We're marching thro' Immanuel's ground to fairer worlds on high.
We're Marching to Zion, by Isaac Watts

People have been singing in worship for centuries. Music is a natural outpouring of our praise to God.

The book of Psalms records songs written and sung as an expression of Israel's worship. Today, Christians enjoy traditional hymns of the faith, as well as the passionate articulation of beliefs expressed in contemporary praise songs. Sometimes the songs are homespun and folksy; sometimes they are sounded through a hundred-voice choir in a cathedral. It makes no difference—whether certain phrases are new or unfamiliar, the beauty of the music and the sentiment of the lyrics expand our worship and lift our souls.

The language of music brings together nations all over the world as they raise their praises to God. Musical styles change and people worship in different languages, but the purpose remains—to praise and bring glory to God's name.

Let our songs abound. Raise your voice... sing!

Read Psalm 98:1–3
Father, I lift my voice in praise to You today.

Blessed Reunion

Friends will be there I have loved long ago; joy like a river around me will flow.
O That Will Be Glory for Me by Charles H. Gabriel

The older you get, the more loved ones you lose to eternity. For all the peace that we feel in knowing that the redeemed of the Lord are now with Him in heaven, we miss them. And truth be told, we might actually feel a bit jealous that while we're here, still struggling in this fallen world, they are in the perfect presence of God.

Our consolation is that the grief and longing we feel are only for a while. The psalmist tells us that a time will come when our labors and trials will be over, and we will be reunited with our friends and family members who preceded us to heaven. Most of all, we will be united with Jesus for eternity. It will be a glorious reunion—a day of untold blessing and unmitigated joy.

Read Matthew 9:8
Remind me, God, that I am heaven-bound and that this time of physical separation is only temporary.

Generous Living

We lift our hearts before you as a token of our love.

HOLY, HOLY by Jimmy Owens

Giving away a favorite possession to a friend is a generous act of selflessness—a sacrifice. It's not human nature, to be sure. But surrendering our own plans or possessions to benefit someone else—to offer the desires of our heart for another's sake—shows our ultimate devotion.

Throughout Scripture, we are reminded that our hearts reveal our true character. When we give our hearts to Christ, we show not only our genuine dedication but also a change of loyalty. Through our active obedience, the Holy Spirit is then able to create within us a pure heart and spirit. God changes us and we can truly serve Him—renewed, restored, and transformed.

God is pleased when we give Him our all in love and devotion. Have you thought about how such a wholehearted commitment will change your life and influence the people around you?

Read Revelation 4:8
I want to worship You with my heart, my head, and my hands, O God.

Win by Forfeit

See from His head, His hands, His feet, sorrow and love flow mingled down.
WHEN I SURVEY THE WONDROUS CROSS by Isaac Watts

To read 1 Corinthians 13 is to realize how much there still is to learn about true love. In the midst of the excruciating pain and sorrow of the cross, Jesus's thoughts were for us. Despite His wounded and bleeding body—despite facing death and humiliation by crucifixion—He asked the Father to grant us mercy for what we were doing to Him. What a phenomenal example of love to emulate!

Christ died so that we might have abundant life. Think on the sorrows Christ bore for us and the love that flowed down from the cross that day—love that embodied patience, kindness, humility, honor, peace, truth, protection, hope, perseverance, and self-sacrifice. Let that love fill and cover your heart. Find opportunities today to emulate Christ, and for God's glory, choose to forgive others.

Read Philippians 1:7
Lord Jesus, help me to follow Your example of love and put others before myself.

God Rules

O let me ne'er forget that though the wrong seems oft so strong, God is the ruler yet.
THIS IS MY FATHER'S WORLD by Maltbie D. Babcock

The media recounts all kinds of stories of illegal behavior, power-hungry leaders, and vulnerable, at-risk children. Bad news has become so prevalent that some folks are choosing not to turn on the nightly news; it's just too disturbing. Who can make sense of the fact that in our world, corrupt behavior sometimes goes unchecked?

Such things cause many people to question God's existence. They ask, "If God is so great and loving, then why is there so much evil in the world? If He's there, wouldn't He do something about it?"

The answer is that evil runs rampant now, but it will not have full sway forever. A day is coming when God will crush all darkness and usher in a new heaven and a new earth. In that day, we will discover what a world without evil looks like.

Until then, the wrong will often seem strong, overwhelming, even impenetrable. But it will not last forever. God is the Ruler of all—now and always.

Read Revelation 21:1–5
One day evil will be destroyed. Until then, keep me focused on You and Your purposes.

The Beauty of Him

Above all powers, above all kings, above all nature and all created things.
ABOVE ALL by Paul Baloche and Lenny LeBlanc

Exploring nature tends to be a favorite pastime of children, whether catching fireflies, poking at slugs, climbing trees, or running after the neighbor's cat. Parents chuckle when their children bring home a new and fascinating discovery. "Can I keep it, please?"

Even as we mature into adulthood, nature seems to bring out our curiosity and draw us deeper. As part of God's creation ourselves, it makes sense that nature would lead us to a personal relationship with our Maker. There is nothing quite like the joy we experience when we understand that the God of the universe—this God who made every living thing around us—is also our own heavenly Father.

Every time you have a moment to notice the world around you today, remind yourself that your Creator is above it all—all the powers, all the kingdoms, and all of nature itself. He is the beginning...and the end. And He chooses to live in and through you.

Read Psalm 24:1–2
I'm so grateful for how You created me and my world, God.

Let Go

I'm putting my fears aside, I'm leaving my doubts behind.
TODAY IS THE DAY by Lincoln Brewster

True confidence comes when we cast off our doubts and fears. But it's not easy. Sometimes even when we think we've conquered a fear, it creeps back in. We panic, forgetting the bold confidence that we once displayed. We slink away, defeated.

When we give our fears and doubts to Jesus, it is important to leave them with Him. Imagine yourself holding a handful of rocks—your doubts and fears—above a rushing river. If you hold them palms up, even if your hand is open wide, you haven't released them. With God's help, turn your palms down, release the rocks, and allow your fears to drop to the surface of the water and disappear beneath it. Don't go in after them. Let them go for good.

Jesus can fill you with hope, confidence, and blessed assurance when you choose to release your burdens and trust in Him.

Read Hebrews 12:1
As I leave my doubts and fears in Your hands, Lord, You take them. Thank You.

Whose Rights?

I'm giving You my dreams; I'm laying down my rights.
Surrender by Marc James

Surrender is not a popular word these days. Instead, culture encourages us to follow our hearts and pursue our dreams. We're told that we're entitled to certain rights and that we should be ready to fight for them. The problem with this philosophy is that in it, we are the ones in control of shaping our own lives.

Scripture teaches something very different from the norm. According to God, we ought to see ourselves as clay in the Potter's hands. He has a beautiful design in mind for our lives and longs to mold us as He sees fit. Unfortunately, our stubborn pride and hardened hearts often get in the way. We buy into the lie that God is out to steal our joy and shatter our dreams. On the contrary, God wants us, His bride, to be completely devoted to Him. This will lead to a deeper intimacy and a more profound joy, but it requires surrender.

Are you willing to give Him your dreams?

Read Jeremiah 18:1–6
Holy Spirit, show me what areas of my heart need to be surrendered today.

Training Exercises

Every joy or testing comes from God above, given to His children as an act of love.
LIKE A RIVER GLORIOUS by Frances Ridley Havergal and Jeff Redd

Obedience training brings to mind puppies lined up with their masters, learning how to behave properly as they walk, eat, and relate to humans. This instruction is necessary because disciplined behavior doesn't come naturally—it's taught.

The Bible tells us that as Christ followers we are trained and corrected as God's beloved children. Learning new behavior patterns from our Father edges us out of our comfort zones. It can be downright painful at times; there's a direct correlation between our response and how persistent and overt the pressure becomes! However, we have an advantage over our pets—we can understand the reason for correction and training. Our loving Father wants to teach us how life works best so we will know how to deal with the obstacles without damaging ourselves and others in the process. He longs to pour blessings into our lives and wants us to know how to identify them.

Read Isaiah 48:18
Lord, thank You for loving me enough to not leave me to my own devices.

Divine Restorations

You are the Potter, I am the clay.
CHANGE MY HEART, O GOD by Eddie Espinosa

In order to make a usable ceramic pot, a ball of soft clay is first put in the middle of a wheel that rapidly turns. With great skill and care, the potter presses and squeezes, gently pulling the clay upward and outward, ultimately shaping it into a functional vessel.

Sound familiar?

Throughout Scripture the analogy of the potter and the clay is used to explain God's ability to mold and shape us into vessels for His purposes. As the Potter, our Redeemer may have to stretch us—even shave off some of the excess. Regardless of how distorted our shape might be, He is divinely skilled; using the tools of grace, time, attention, and love, He forms us into useful instruments.

When we go to Christ with a request to change our hearts, we must humbly submit to the refining ministry of the Holy Spirit—and become like pliable lumps of clay being readied upon the potter's wheel.

Read Isaiah 64:8

Holy Spirit, I submit myself to Your refining touch; do as You will.

Great Expectations

In the Cross, in the Cross, be my glory ever, till my raptured soul shall find rest beyond the river.
NEAR THE CROSS by Fanny J. Crosby

As competitive beings we seek recognition and credit for our accomplishments. It's not long, however, before we discover that earthly success is elusive and short-lived. Unfortunately, many of us soon become jaded in our pursuit of praise.

As believers, Christ is our glory and the cross a promise that one day all weariness will vanish in the twinkling of an eye. At our Lord's return, Gabriel's trumpet shall sound and we will exchange this temporary existence for eternity with the Savior. Eternity, where our souls will find nothing but rest and fulfillment.

In the meantime, as we labor in Jesus's name to reach others with the Good News of the gospel, we can stand near the cross, find our joy in its message of redemption, and look forward with anticipation to resting in His glory.

Read Isaiah 41:18
Thank You, God, that I have the hope of rest in You.

Fired Up!

Give us passion for Your name. Jesus light the flame.
GLORIFY by Linda Barnhill

They say the two things you should never publicly discuss are religion and politics. Why are they such hot topics? What is it about these matters that provokes people, even friends, to "come to blows" about their personal perspectives? It's passion.

As human beings, we get zealous about what means the most to us. For some, it's art. Many are die-hard sports fans. And yet others are dedicated to family. When it comes to these things, we take a stand because we have a passion for them.

In parts of today's world, people with a passion for Christ are still being martyred. In Luke 12, Jesus says that He came to bring fire; that people would be divided, even within families. Jesus calls us to choose whom we will follow. To glorify God is to be passionate about serving Him.

Read Matthew 28:18–19
Lord Jesus, make me a fanatical follower.

Hide and Seek

Jesus sought me when a stranger, wandering from the fold of God.
Come Thou Fount of Every Blessing by Robert Robinson

Some of us have lived in homes where the occupants were basically strangers. It may have been a new-roommate situation where only physical space and expenses were shared and nothing beyond common courtesy was expected or necessary. Other times, painful dysfunction causes relatives (who should have a special bond) to disconnect and isolate themselves from their family members.

Why did Jesus seek us when we were strangers and welcome us in as kin? Because we were created to be a part of His eternal family. It's our sin that drove us to hide in shame and hang a DO NOT DISTURB sign on the doors of our hearts. Like a dad waiting up for a teen out past curfew, Father God's relentless love won't rest until we're safely home, reconciled to the family and secure. In response to His Father's longing, Jesus came looking for us.

Read Proverbs 10:22
Jesus, thank You for searching for me, even when I wasn't looking for You.

Responding to Suffering

Then all hurt and pain will cease, and we'll be with Him forever.
THERE IS A DAY by Nathan Fellinghamm

Anguish is an inevitable part of life. It doesn't matter if we are rich or poor, black or white, young or old. No one is exempt! It's hard to understand. When we run into trauma and tragedy, we ask ourselves, "Where's God?"

When He created the world, God did not intend for us to experience suffering. It wasn't part of His plan. However, we now live with the consequences of sinful choices. And when we read our Bibles, we see that God used the distress of people like Joseph, Job, and Jesus to further His sovereign plan.

Glory to God, we have hope! While distress is inherited from the sins of the world's first man and woman, Jesus's death on the cross atoned for that original sin. Through Jesus's resurrection and His promise to return, we know that one day He will put an end to all sorrow and pain. And in the meantime, though anguish may come, our response must be to turn to God and believe that in our pain, He will accomplish His good purpose.

Read 1 Thessalonians 4:17
I love You, Jesus, and I trust that this pain I am experiencing is for Your glory.

Higher Power

Simply trusting Thee, Lord Jesus, I behold Thee as Thou art.
Jesus, I Am Resting, Resting by Jean Sophia Pigott

Mother Teresa once said, "I know God will not give me anything I can't handle. I just wish He didn't trust me so much."

Have you ever felt that way? There's no question that keeping the faith can be tough, especially during times of adversity. Exhaustion sets in, yet we can't sleep. God is silent, yet He expects us to rest in Him. It is at these critical crossroads that our faith is stretched. But if we will persevere, God will create in us a new level of spiritual strength. And we will understand more of who He is—and who we are in Him.

Remember, you are a child of the King, the offspring of a sovereign heavenly Father. You have power from on high! Carry that confidence with you into this day.

Read Psalm 9:10
As I place my life in Your hands, give me the faith to wait on You, God.

Confronting Pain

Praise Him for His grace and favor to our fathers in distress.
PRAISE, MY SOUL, THE KING OF HEAVEN by Henry F. Lyte

Stephen was stoned. James the Just was beaten to death with a club. Peter was crucified upside down. Bartholomew was beaten with rods and then crucified. Thomas was killed with a spear. Paul was beheaded. Each of these men faced horrible pain with great courage, rejoicing that they were counted worthy to suffer for their faith. In each of their situations, God gave them the grace and assurance they needed to endure the pain.

In this life, we will sometimes have to face terrible pain. When challenged with suffering, we wonder how to find the strength to continue. But our God is the same yesterday, today, and forever. The God who gave these men—our spiritual "fathers"—the grace to meet death is the same God we serve today.

When pain crosses your path, ask God for help, and He will give you the grace, favor, and strength to persevere.

Read Acts 5:41
Lord, I thank You that You are strong enough for my pain.

June 11

Creation Appreciation

Your mighty works displayed for all to see.
BEAUTIFUL ONE by Tim Hughes

The order and beauty of creation is astounding. If our planet was anywhere else in the solar system, we would not be able to study nature with the same accuracy and enjoyment. According to *The Privileged Planet* by Guillermo Gonzalez and Jay Richards, "The conditions allowing for intelligent life on Earth also make our planet strangely well suited for viewing and analyzing the universe." We have the best location in our solar system to view eclipses, and we have one of the best places in our galaxy from which to view the other planets, stars, and moons.

God clearly wants us to see the beauty of His mighty works. From the largest galaxies to the smallest seashells, every part of His creation has purpose. Looking over the edge of a mountain or watching a sunset paint the sky teaches us about God's artistic mastery. The more we learn about our surroundings, the more we appreciate God's glory.

Read Psalm 145:3–7
I stand in awe, Lord, at the beauty of Your creation.

Unified in Him

So we lift up holy hands in one accord.
BLESSED BE THE NAME OF THE LORD by Don Moen

A young man watched from the corner of the dim room as the lookout let another missionary into the secret meeting. When everyone had arrived, they formed a circle and knelt together. One man told of a cult that had persecuted his church. When he finished his story, another told of how he feared for his congregation because some members were being threatened by government officials. Every minister spoke, each sharing his own story of opposition. Eventually, they were overcome and pressed their faces to the ground, weeping, and began to pray aloud. Amid their desperate cries for protection, praise and worship flowed from their lips. Fear and anxiety melted away as praise centered their hearts on the One that brought them together.

God was present at that meeting, just as He is with us today. When two or more gather in His name, He is there. Come together and lift up holy hands in one accord. He will be in attendance too.

Read Matthew 18:20
Lord, thank You for coming into our presence.

June 13

Worthy of Awe

He reigns from heav'n above with wisdom, pow'r and love.
AWESOME GOD by Rich Mullens

When David's son Solomon became king of Israel, God gave Him a great gift—the opportunity to ask for anything he wanted and have his wish granted. Solomon asked for wisdom. God commended him for this choice, giving him power and many riches as well. Solomon became the wisest man ever to live, but later in life he turned away from God to worship the false gods of his wives.

Despite Solomon's great wisdom—perhaps even because of it—he fell prey to pride, depending on his own intellect rather than relying on God's wisdom and judgment. Even the greatest and wisest humans fall short of God's standards of holiness. He is the only one who can reign with true wisdom, power, and love. Your King, your Savior, reigns over your life with these three important qualities. What does it mean to you today that He is wise, powerful, and loving?

Read Psalm 48:1
Lord, You are worthy of all praise. I praise You for Your awesomeness.

Wounded Healer

Trusting only in Thy merit, would I seek Thy face.
Heal my wounded, broken spirit, save me by Thy grace.
Pass Me Not, O Gentle Savior by Fanny J. Crosby

Every person we encounter has a story—and many of those stories include great pain. If we only knew the number of wounded, broken spirits that surround us! No one goes through this life untouched by loss, grief, fear, or worry, no matter what their life looks like on the outside.

What about you today? Are you wounded? Are you lost in the darkness of a pain you can't describe, a hurt that no one seems to understand? In those moments when you feel broken beyond repair, it is hard to know where to turn. Hope disappears and words of comfort fall flat. It is in those moments of despair that we must especially seek God, trusting that He is able to carry us through.

Search for His face and get to know Him in a deeper way. He too has been wounded and broken. He has experienced pain beyond description so that we won't have to suffer forever. It is through His wounds that you can be healed.

Read Isaiah 53:4–5
Lord, when all hope seems lost, remind me of Your grace and healing.

Taste the Goodness

This is my daily bread; Your very word spoken to me.
<small>BREATHE</small> by Marie Barnett

The types of bread we have available to us are countless. Baguette. Brioche. Challa. Pan dulce. Tortilla. Wonderful flavors from all over the world—from bland to spicy to sweet—tempt our taste buds. Fun shapes and sizes charm us to sample and savor the goodness.

Though bread has great versatility, one thing remains true of it in all its forms: bread is a staple of life worldwide. A daily helping of bread (or the grain bread is made from) contributes to our physical well-being. It assures our diet is balanced and nutritious.

The Word of God does the same for our spirits. It sustains us daily. It balances busy lives and packed agendas. It nourishes our spirits during trials. It fills us with God's love, peace, joy.

Jesus's Word gives us a taste of God's goodness. It satisfies our spiritual hunger. And taking it in daily makes us want more of it. Our spiritual daily bread is the appetizer to a veritable feast. Are you ready to eat?

Read Matthew 4:4
Lord, help me to crave Your Word as I do food.

Wait on Him

Strength will rise as we wait upon the Lord.
EVERLASTING GOD by Brenton Brown and Ken Riley

Those who finish a cross-country race provide ideal examples of athletes that have run a good race and are now spent. Some runners collapse; others are on the verge of collapse after crossing the finish line. Because they've given their all during the demanding race, they need time to regain their normal breathing, rehydrate, and cool down after having exhausted themselves of mental and physical resources.

As Christians, we too need to take time out from the race of life and be renewed by breathing the spiritual air of God's presence and drinking from the well of His Word. Otherwise we may be in danger of spiritual collapse. Tapping in to what the Lord offers us refreshes our spirits.

Are you weary or weak? Breathe deeply, soak in His Word, and wait upon Him.

Read Isaiah 40:31
Renew my strength, heavenly Father, so that I may soar on wings like eagles.

Surrender

I'll stand, my soul, Lord, to You surrendered.
THE STAND by Joel Houston

Winston Churchill once declared, "We shall never surrender!" He was, of course, referring to his country's position in World War II, but we all have said—or thought—the same thing. Surrender isn't a word we want in our vocabulary. Few of us are willing to succumb to defeat, much less relinquish control of our existence.

Surrendering our lives to Jesus requires that we give up command of our time, possessions, and free will. We give Him jurisdiction of what we consider to be our "rights." We acknowledge that what is ours really belongs to God. We are merely caretakers of the gifts He has given us.

This is not surrender that ends in loss, like an army giving in to an enemy. This is abandonment that leads to peace, joy, and fulfillment. When we hand over our lives to Jesus, He blesses us with all of Himself in return.

Soul surrender equals ultimate victory.

Read Luke 9:24–25
Show me how to surrender completely to You, God.

Our God Reigns!

Let the redeemed of the Lord sing, Our God reigns!
RISE AND SING by Steve Fee

Do you ever feel despair when you think of all that's wrong with the world? Do you ever wonder where God is in the midst of the mess we've created? Theologically, you know God is King, but where is the evidence that He reigns?

In Psalm 107, the writer urges those whom God has redeemed to tell their story: to tell how God led the wanderer home; how He freed those imprisoned by their sin; how He calmed the sea and brought forth life in the midst of drought-stricken lands.

What about you? Has God intervened in your life and done what you were helpless to do? Tell your story! Yes, terrible things are happening in our world, but in the midst of all the brokenness, our God is still in the business of healing, restoring, and freeing. We have a King, and He reigns!

Read Psalm 107:2, 10–16
Help me encourage others, Lord, with the story of Your grace in my life

Secured by Grace

There's an anchor for my soul. I can say, "It is well."
I WILL RISE by Louie Giglio, Chris Tomlin, Matt Maher, and Jesse Reeves

In the midst of deep grief over the unexpected, tragic death of his teenage son, a father managed to continue to get out of bed every day, go to work, attend church, and parent his other children. It was during this time of overwhelming and unspeakable pain that he discovered firsthand that he was being sustained. Upheld by the steadying hand of a loving heavenly Father.

A soul that is anchored in the Lord is not easily tossed about by life's inevitable crises. The faith of the anchored believer holds steady in the storms of life—not by its own doing but because the anchor is the Almighty God Himself. So today, rest assured that if you have placed your faith in God, He is with you. Whatever adversity you may encounter, God loves and secures you; through Him, you can endure any situation.

Read Hebrews 6:19–20
I set my mind like a flint, dear God, knowing that my destiny is anchored in You

Out of the Darkness

Into the marvelous light I'm running, out of darkness, out of shame.
MARVELOUS LIGHT by Charlie Hall

In Mark Twain's *Tom Sawyer*, Tom and Becky get lost in a cave, their candle sputtering out and leaving them in pitch-black darkness for several days. But oh, the glorious joy when they emerge into daylight again!

Scripture often refers to life outside of God as darkness. Whether due to ignorance—for the Bible also says we were "lost"—or to shameful disobedience, we wander helplessly in that gloom, until the light of the gospel illuminates our path at last. Leaving behind the shame that accrues with sin, we run toward the light at last. Behind us: confusion, fear, and shame. Ahead: clarity, security, and perfect restoration. Coming into the light, we find that Jesus not only forgives us; He completely forgets our disobedience and shame. It's like a bad dream evaporating in morning's sunlight.

Leave the darkness and run—truly run—into His marvelous light.

Read Ephesians 5:7–17
Thank You for making a way for me to come to You, Lord.

Anchored

When darkness veils His lovely face, I rest on His unchanging grace.
My Hope Is Built on Nothing Less by Edward Mote

Waiting for an answer to prayer can be exhausting. It requires endurance; yet in the long run, it strengthens our faith and becomes the stuff personal testimonies are made of. Thankfully, we can turn to Scripture for reassurance as we wait. It is rich with testimonies of God's grace and immeasurable love for His people in their time of need, teaching us that we have a reliable heavenly Father and giving us hope when the waiting time becomes taxing.

We serve an all-powerful, all-knowing God whose character is unchanging, unlimited by time or space. But His time is not our time; His ways are not always our own. Waiting forces us to rest in Him, trusting that He will be faithful and that He has our best interests in mind.

God's proven nature is the foundation on which we can build our lives and place our hope. When the way seems dark, when we wrestle with uncertainty, our souls can rest in God and not be shaken.

Read Psalm 125:1
Just knowing You are there sustains me, Lord.

Faithful amid Change

You're unchangeable; You're unshakeable; You're unstoppable.

You Are God Alone (Not a God) by Billy Foote and Cindy Foote

Our world is constantly changing. Our grandparents could not have imagined the technology we have at our disposal. Laptop computers, smart phones, and DVRs—all were unheard of even thirty short years ago. Likewise, our grandchildren will be using devices that are inconceivable to us today.

In the midst of constant change, we have assurance of a God who remains the same. His character and very nature remain constant. In spite of changes that have occurred in the world since the beginning of time, our God is no less just, holy, or sovereign than He ever has been. His promises and plans for us do not change. While we may change our minds or feelings toward others (and sometimes toward God Himself!), our heavenly Father feels the same way toward us as He did when He sent Jesus to die on the cross for our sins. He loved us yesterday, loves us today, and will love us tomorrow.

Read Malachi 3:6

Thank You for being an unchanging God in a changing world.

Ultimate Guidance

Where You lead us we'll follow all the way.

AWESOME IS THE LORD MOST HIGH by Chris Tomlin, Jesse Reeves, Cary Pierce, and Jon Abel

Before the first transcontinental flight was flown or unmanned satellites were even imagined, our awesome God had a divine GPS system up and running. He's always known the exact distance between where you are and where you need to be, and the best route for getting there.

When we familiarize ourselves with the Word through reading and study, the Holy Spirit will use Scripture to alert us when we've made a wrong turn, gone down a dead-end street, or require an alternate route.

Spending time daily in God's Word will help equip you to navigate your life's journey and follow as the Lord leads. Pray today and ask the Father to bring verses to your mind and heart just when you need them to guide you through uncharted territory or make a course correction.

Read Isaiah 57:14

Lord, please don't be my copilot; be my pilot, so that I can follow the course You set.

Ever Present

Blessed Redeemer, Emmanuel. The Rescue for sinners, the Ransom from heaven.
Jesus Messiah by Daniel Carson, Chris Tomlin, Ed Cash, and Jesse Reeves

Naming a child is a significant event. It can carry the weight of a family's heritage, not to mention parental aspirations. Hidden in the meaning of the name may be the family's religious beliefs, political affiliations, cultural background, creative impulses, hopes, and dreams. It's often a nod to the past as well as a glimpse of the future.

Emmanuel, a name given centuries ago to Jesus at the angel's instruction to Joseph, still means the same thing today: God is with us. Nothing changes the promise of His name—regardless of what we face. He laughs and cries with us, walks beside us, and watches over as we sleep through the night.

He's present at every birth, wedding, baptism, home going, and celebration.

Knowing God is with us changes our outlook on life, making it possible to enjoy the many daily blessings we receive. Seek and you will find that God is in everything you do today.

Read Matthew 1:23
Let me recognize Your presence here and now, Lord.

Soul Renovator

He restoreth my soul when I'm weary; He giveth me strength day by day.
SURELY GOODNESS AND MERCY by John W. Peterson and Alfred B. Smith

Severe trials will come. The death of a relationship. Loss. Illness. Devastating disappointment. At some point, we all encounter the worst we can imagine. And the battle soon becomes long and tiresome. We grow so puzzled as we wait for divine intervention and healing that we weaken and often surrender to anxiety and fear.

In uncertain times, we are especially vulnerable to the lies of Satan. Yet in the midst of uncertainty, there is a truth to which we may cling: Jehovah has not abandoned us. God provides a way station for the weary. Our heavenly Father is a dawn bringer—overcoming dark nights. Jesus understands suffering and sorrow—He is the almighty Source from which we can draw strength.

He will rescue you, cover you, and restore your soul. Are you tired? Weary? Confused? Come to Jesus.

Read Psalm 23
Lord Jesus, sustain and revive me through the power of Your love.

Strong Spirit

Strengthen me, Holy Spirit, to defend what is holy.
PRAYER OF ST. AUGUSTINE by Mark Dicristina

The Holy Spirit, our promised Advocate who came to dwell with us after Jesus's return to heaven, supplies us with so many things—comfort, guidance, courage. He is with us, helping us learn as we read the Bible and ministering to us when we are in need. He gives us the wisdom to answer questions about our faith, and then softens the hearts of those who are willing to listen so they are more receptive to the gospel message. He also gives us the power to defend holiness in an unholy world, and to live rightly ourselves.

Today, allow the Holy Spirit to give you the strength that you need to face whatever comes your way. To stand for righteousness, to defend the truth, to hold strong in the face of adversity. For Him.

Read John 14:26–27
Holy Spirit, work through me so that I might be strong when I feel weak.

Just as I Am

Just as I am, Thou wilt receive, wilt welcome, pardon,
cleanse, relieve; because Thy promise I believe.

JUST AS I AM by Charlotte Elliot

"Come as you are." If we received an invitation to a gathering and were told, "It's casual," or, "Come as you are," we would certainly still prep ourselves to look our best. We would shower, wash our hair, brush our teeth, and put on clean clothing. After all, we don't want anyone to see us as our smelly, dirty, unkempt selves—you know, the real us.

Christ has issued an invitation, and it says, "Come as you are." And He really means it. There's no image to maintain—He knows us. He's seen us at our worst. We don't have to clean ourselves up first to come into His presence. We don't have to overcome some sin, or wait until we're better people or become more worthy of His company. Instead, we can come—foul, corrupt, messy, sinful, addicted, sad, resentful, bitter—and let Jesus do His work in us. He welcomes, pardons, cleanses, relieves, and provides for us.

Do you believe it? Come as you are. Let Him work in you.

Read Isaiah 55:1

Lord, You draw me close, just as I am. I praise You!

Likeness

Over every thought, over every word, may my life reflect the beauty of my Lord.

Lord, Reign in Me by Brenton Brown

Reflections. Many of us avoid mirrors because we dislike something about our physical appearance. Some of us are drawn to them, unable to stop admiring our reflection. Most of us are somewhere in between.

But Scripture refers to our reflection as more of an inner mirror than an outer one. Perhaps that's why Scripture reminds us that "as [a man] thinks in his heart, so is he" (Proverbs 23:7 NKJV). In 2 Timothy, we're told to guard our hearts and minds. So we must ask ourselves: What occupies our minds? What do we let in that is reflecting out?

It may seem impossible to limit what gets inside us. But what we let inside our minds is a choice. The apostle Paul instructs us to take control of our thought life. Rather than entertain ungodly thoughts, we are to cast them down, bringing them in line with Christ. On the other hand, considering those things that are good and pure and holy will reflect the beauty that is our Lord.

Read 2 Corinthians 10:5
Father, help me to turn away every thought that is not of You.

Only the Beginning

By His death I live again.
THE GOSPEL SONG by Drew Jones

We mourn the finality of death because, as mortal human beings, it's hard for our limited minds to wrap themselves around the concept of eternity. Most of what we know has a beginning and an end. For this reason, we can understand the grief of Mary and Martha at the death of their brother. Even though they knew Jesus—and believed He was the Messiah—it didn't occur to them that Lazarus could be resurrected and his life restored. Miraculously, our Lord did the seemingly impossible and brought him back to life.

Book by book, the New Testament testifies that because of Jesus Christ's sacrifice, we are in a way restored, "brought back to life." And better yet, we're free to live our lives more abundantly here on earth.

When it's over, death for the believer is really only a moment. As difficult as it is for us to imagine, we can celebrate that to be absent from our earthly body is to be present with our Creator.

Read John 11:4
Jesus, thank You for enduring death—so we don't have to.

In the Eye of the Beholder

You're awesome in beauty, greatly to be praised.
GLORIOUS AND MIGHTY by Joel Sczebel, Todd Twining, and Bob Kauflin

The beauty business is a booming, multi-billion-dollar enterprise. It promises to remove every physical flaw imaginable—even the inevitable signs of aging. If we believed the hype, we'd think makeup and skin treatments were the only way to loveliness.

Granted, such things may improve our looks, but they can't cover up hearts scarred by sin. They can't remove the signs of heartache. Nor can they cleanse our thoughts or purify our minds.

But God can. In His great holiness, our God powerfully transforms hearts and lives, giving us a "makeover" in His image. His Word, in our lives and on our lips, enhances our innermost beings, renews our souls, and helps us exude His grace and loving-kindness.

God beautifies from the inside out. Made in His image, we reflect His awesome beauty when we mirror His ways. No makeup required.

Read Psalm 96
Father, please help others to see Your beauty, not my flaws.

Nothing but the Blood

Nothing can for sin atone.... Naught of good that I have done—nothing but the blood of Jesus.
NOTHING BUT THE BLOOD by Robert Lowry

When asked to think of somebody who has spent their life "doing good," who comes to mind? Mother Teresa? A grandparent? A Sunday school teacher? Many people do good things—some volunteer at local soup kitchens, others facilitate the neighborhood watch, and still others run errands for shut-ins. Yet not all of these "do-gooders" are Christians. They make moral, generous choices simply because they know it's the right thing to do, not because they've chosen what Jesus would do.

It's true that no one needs Jesus in order to do good. If a person wants to be saved, however, they do need Him. Merely doing good things doesn't get any of us to heaven. We are all sinners, and we can never be good enough or do enough to enter the heavenly gates on our own.

Nothing can atone for our sins—nothing but the blood of Jesus.

Read Hebrews 9:11–14
Thank You, Jesus, for the blood You shed for me.

Paid in Full

'Tis done, the great transaction's done—I am my Lord's and He is mine.
O HAPPY DAY! by Philip Doddridge

Transactions are typically financial deals—someone buys, someone sells. And particularly with clearance items, sales are often final. Thank goodness that's the case with our salvation—Jesus paid the price of our redemption once and for all on the cross. As our almighty Savior, He did what only He could do: He conquered death and the grave, securing our eternal fellowship with Him. That is worth celebrating!

Now, think about it. What do you do when you get something that improves your life? Typically, we share the information with friends and coworkers—or even better, they can see for themselves, by our demeanor and attitude, that we've got something good going on.

How is the gospel changing your day-to-day life? Do you function differently than others? Can they see the change that redemption makes in your life? Are you living worthy of the gospel? After all, it's a big deal.

Read Isaiah 25:9

Jesus, You paid the price to make me a child of God. Remind me to share my joy with others.

Focused on Jesus

Look to Him, your Savior, in temptation's hour.
At the Name of Jesus by Caroline M. Noel

Facebook. Chips and soda. A beautiful woman. A new pair of shoes. Each of these, on its own, seems innocent enough, yet depending on the situation, they can altogether represent genuine temptation. The urge to waste time instead of working. The craving for junk food while on a strict diet. The desire for someone other than a spouse. The impulse purchase while on a strict budget—each is an attack on a vulnerable target.

Jesus was tempted by the enemy. In Luke we see that Satan and his forces sought to appeal to Jesus's desires on all fronts.

Fortunately for us, He remained steadfast, unmovable. Jesus was not swayed by the devil's urgings. We don't have to be either.

We can resist temptation. Gratefully, the Bible promises in 1 Corinthians 10:13 that God will not allow us to be tempted beyond what we are able to bear. He will provide us with a way of escape. All we have to do is use it!

Read Luke 4:12–13
Strengthen my resolve, God, until all my faculties are focused only on You.

Wave Your Flag!

His banner over us is love, our sword the Word of God.
FAITH IS THE VICTORY by John H. Yates

Every Fourth of July we celebrate US independence by marching in parades, waving the American flag, and exploding fireworks. Our flag, also known as "Old Glory," serves as a symbol of freedom and independence for all Americans. For decades, it has signified the country's victory over those who endeavored to keep us bound.

In the book of Exodus, Moses spoke about another, more important banner: "Moses built an altar and called it The Lord is my Banner" (Exodus 17:15 NIV). The prophet Isaiah said that the banner of God is Jesus (Isaiah 11:1–12). David explains in Psalm 60:4 that the banner will be given to those who believe in God.

In times of conflict, despair, and uncertainty, turn to Jehovah-Nissi—the "Lord your Banner"—to fight your battles and free you from bondage. Whatever the struggle, the banner of God can bring victory—through Christ's work on our behalf.

Read 1 John 5:4
Teach me to walk under the banner of Your protection and love.

Christ's Fireworks

It may be at midday; it may be at twilight. It may be, perchance,
that the blackness of midnight will burst into light in the blaze of His glory.
CHRIST RETURNETH by H. L. Turner

Every year Americans spend millions of dollars on fireworks. Children wave sparklers in the night air and grown men set off rockets, while mothers and wives stand by, watching with anxious delight. The sounds of distant rumblings fill the air like faraway drums or gunshots, and the sky is lit with a blaze of colors, the emblem of a nationwide celebration of freedom.

Someday Christ will return to earth, and the sky will be lit with all of His glory. As awed as we are by fireworks, they will pale in comparison to the jaw-dropping, brilliant display we will see on that day. Jesus will triumphantly appear with great splendor to gather His bride, the Church. Until then, our annual fireworks displays can remind us to pray for His swift return and watch for His coming glory.

Keep an eye on the horizon...and be ready. It will be a wonderful show!

Read Matthew 24:44
Lord, come quickly!

Did You Know?

Creation shows Your splendor, Your reigning majesty.
How Excellent Is Thy Name by Paul Smith, Dick Tunney, and Melodie Tunney

How is this for creative diversity? Alligators can live up to at least one year without eating. Asparagus takes about eighteen months to grow before it's ready to harvest. Among the twenty thousand types of bees, only four make honey. Eighty percent of the animals that live on Madagascar can only be found there. In Asia alone, there are more than 125 different kinds of maple trees.

God's creativity and splendor, exhibited through His creation, is incredible. The complexity of just one of His creations is so far beyond our understanding that we can't duplicate it—even with all our technology.

Indeed, the world around us demonstrates His supernatural skill. Yet the Bible tells us that His eye is on the sparrow as well. He cares in such detail that He dresses even the lilies of the field.

The miraculous way in which the universe functions—on grand levels and at atomic levels—is a credit to His power, His sovereignty, His love. Aren't you grateful that's the God you serve?

Read Psalm 148:13
Creator God, thank You for the witness of Your creation.

A Sure Thing

Come to this fountain so rich and sweet; cast your poor soul at the Savior's feet.
Down at the Cross by Elisha A. Hoffman

For generations, numerous cultures around the world have shared the tradition of wishing wells, viewing them as sources of good luck. The ancients threw coins into a wishing well in an attempt to gain favor from the gods.

Thankfully, as believers in Christ Jesus, we have a hope that is rooted in truth instead of coincidence or chance. Because of our great Savior and the power of His work on the cross, we have access to the living water that satisfies our desires. We are able to shed our sins, concerns, and burdens at His altar and gain an overwhelming sense of peace that can only come from a loving Redeemer.

The apostle Paul wrote that there is nothing we can do in the flesh to create our salvation. It's not a matter of luck—it's grace. Amazing grace. How fortunate we are!

Read Galatians 2:20
Father God, thank You for providing salvation that is certain for all who will accept it.

Restored

Now hear me while I pray; take all my guilt away. O let me from this day be wholly Thine!
My Faith Looks Up to Thee by Ray Palmer

It is human nature to want things to be made whole. We like to travel full circle and experience closure. God gives us that desire—and that very experience—through Him. When we have failed Him, He allows us a means to be made whole again via the road to forgiveness. That road starts with spending time with God. In prayer, we can talk to God about anything, including things we need to confess. When Jesus forgives our sins, restoration is complete. Every time.

The process of being made whole begins with repentance—true sorrow over our mistakes and a willingness to change our behavior. Then come the blessings of reconciliation and transformation.

Christ can make you whole in a moment. Not by some sudden change in your feelings but by taking charge of your life and filling it with His Spirit. Jesus brought redemption to a broken world. His sacrifice made it possible for our relationship with God to be restored. Seek Him this day.

Read Ephesians 1:7
Reconcile me to You, O God.

Searchlight

Search me, try me, consume all my darkness.
SHINE, JESUS, SHINE by Graham Kendrick

For more than forty years the medical technology of the CT scan has had an impact on patients' lives. The ability to see inside a patient's body without exploratory surgery and gain a detailed perspective of how things are functioning has greatly aided the process of diagnosis and treatment. The capacity to conduct such in-depth analysis has made the difference between sickness and health for millions of patients.

Most of us would not voluntarily subject ourselves to such an assessment if we were feeling great. Yet that's exactly what's necessary spiritually. Because we're born selfish, when left to govern ourselves, we lose perspective and our sinful nature grows out of control. We need the light of a holy Savior to expose our immorality and destructive predisposition to ego. By accepting Jesus's probing, illuminative, redemptive work, we invite Him to lead us to a life more abundant.

Read John 12:46
Hallelujah, the light of Jesus lives in me.

WWJD

Fill me with life anew, that I may love what Thou dost love and do what Thou wouldst do.
BREATHE ON ME, BREATH OF GOD by Elizabeth C. Clephane

Remember the acronym WWJD—What Would Jesus Do? Chances are, you've seen these letters printed on everything from coffee mugs to bumper stickers. If only figuring out the answer was as easy as writing out those letters!

Fortunately, there is help for when you're wondering what Jesus would do—or what He would have you do. First, spend time with Him in His Word. Study how He acted and reacted as a citizen of the world; explore what He said about how to treat others. Then spend time talking to Him and seeking His guidance. Finally, take what He shows you and act on it. Before long, you'll be doing as Jesus did: actively loving and serving others. And then they'll see Jesus through you!

Read 1 John 2:6
Lord, guide me to live in such a way that others will see You, not me.

Big Bark, Little Bite

So shall I be saved from my enemies.
I Will Call Upon the Lord by Michael O'Shields

Enemies were easy to identify when we were in school. They talked about us behind our backs, celebrated when we messed up, and did their best to make sure others shared their opinion of us. Now that we're adults, our enemies may be more subtle, more subversive. But we're still likely to face opposition.

We believers battle an unseen enemy, but an enemy nonetheless—one who hates the very ground we walk on. He lies to us; he seeks to trap us. And not only does he wait for us to mess up, but he strategically places obstacles in our way to make us stumble. His name is Satan.

But next time you're tempted to worry about him, just remember: God is far greater. And He has assured you that victory can be yours.

Read Psalm 18:3
Lord, help me remember that Satan can do no more than You allow.

July 12

Unselfish Savior

But drops of grief can ne'er repay the debt of love I owe.
ALAS! AND DID MY SAVIOR BLEED by Isaac Watts

The prophet Isaiah foretold that Jesus would suffer on the cross: "He was wounded for our transgressions...and by His stripes we are healed" (Isaiah 53:5 NKJV). In Hebrew, the word wounded means "to pierce" or "to puncture." Jesus was pierced through, bled, and died for our sins. He suffered and was sacrificed so that we might be healed.

The harsh and brutal suffering our Savior endured was not simply so that we might receive physical healing; He endured it so we could be spiritually redeemed. God loves us so much that He was willing to sacrifice His Son in order to restore us, body and soul. The Father laid upon Jesus the sins and iniquities of us all, and it is because of His unselfish choice that we have salvation. No act of love has ever been greater!

Read Isaiah 53:5
Jesus, thank You for allowing Yourself to be wounded for me.

Facing Goliaths

Never a heartache and never a groan, never a teardrop and never a moan;
never a danger, but there on the throne.
Moment by Moment by Daniel W. Whittle

Margaret had fought cancer before, but this time it had returned with a vengeance. The disease had metastasized to the bones in her back, requiring fourteen hours of surgery, a twenty-four-day stay in the hospital, multiple radiation treatments, and numerous rounds of chemotherapy. Throughout the process of daily shots and blood infusions, this beloved grandmother and longtime follower of Christ discovered anew what it meant to trust God moment by moment. As her battle continued, Margaret felt the embrace of her Lord—she was under His tender care. God's presence was tangible; it was as if He was sitting by her side through her every moment. And in reality, He was!

Your battle might not be cancer this day, but do you sense Him near you? He is with you, regardless of the Goliath you face.

Read Mark 14:35–36
Dear God, moment by moment, teach us to trust in Your unfailing care for us!

Home to Him

How lovely is Your dwelling place, O Lord Almighty.
BETTER IS ONE DAY by Matt Redman

Is it possible to find God? This is one of the most-asked questions since Adam and Eve were driven from the garden. People have gone on pilgrimages, families have divided, and nations have warred in their search for the answer.

Thankfully, God has provided a resounding answer. In Ephesians, we are reminded of this awesome fact of grace: God lives in His people. Indeed, Jesus promised that where two or three gather in His name, He will join them.

Praise the Lord! God chooses to come and live among people who offer up themselves to Him. Through His Holy Spirit, He miraculously forms us into His dwelling place. What a privilege!

Read Ephesians 2:22
We are blessed that You choose to dwell within us, Father.

Firm Foundation

Could my tears forever flow, could my zeal no languor know,
these for sin could not atone—Thou must save, and Thou alone.

ROCK OF AGES by Augustus M. Toplady

When something is said to be "as solid as a rock," you know that it can withstand pressure. Lots of pressure. Which is why the Bible warns us to build our lives on "the solid rock" (Matthew 7:24–27). This rock, or foundation, is Jesus—God's one and only Son. God's church is built on that same foundation, and according to Jesus in Matthew, not even the gates of hell can prevail against it.

When we've got that kind of a foundation—one that neither dynamite nor the enemy can destroy—who are we to fear? We can hide behind our Rock. Take shelter in His strength. Rest within the security He provides.

Maybe life's a little crazy right now. Maybe you're feeling unsettled, unsure. Cling not to the things of this lost and ever-changing world but to the Rock of Ages—the Rock that is higher and stronger and surer than you and I. Cling to Jesus!

Read Psalm 61:2
I am holding on to You, Jesus.

The Ultimate Reunion

For His returning we watch and we pray.
Sing to the King by Billy Foote and Charles Silvester Horne

We've all seen at least one television talk show in which family members, childhood friends, or long-lost loves are joyfully reunited after decades of separation. In some cases, people wait for years to be with their loved ones again, while other people never get that opportunity.

Take a minute and imagine the person you most want to meet or see again. What would you do to prepare for such a reunion? Buy a new outfit? Arrange a time to introduce them to your friends? Or make notes about everything you want to ask or say?

In the same way, how are you preparing for the return of Jesus? Scripture promises that He will return for His bride, the church. Although the day and time of His coming is unknown, will you be ready? Are you excited that your Savior may arrive at any moment—just as He promised? Are you ready now?

Read Matthew 24:42
Lord, make me ready to meet You in the sky.

The Light That Leads

You are the love that frees us. You are the light that leads us.
Sing, Sing, Sing by Chris Tomlin, Jesse Reeves, Matt Gilder, Daniel Carson, and Travis Nunn

"Relationship" and "freedom": two things we all long for because both were lost, at least in part, in Eden. At the first bite of forbidden fruit, humanity's relationship with our Creator, as well as our relationship with fellow human beings, was broken. And in that moment, our freedom was wrenched away by our own act of disobedience and replaced with the shackles of slavery to sin. But love won out. Love stooped down to our level of fallen misery and pursued us all the way to the cross. Love freed us to live again in right relationship with God and with one another.

Maybe you're seeking relationships and freedom in the wrong places. Or maybe you're trying to please God by following rules, out of fear of punishment. God accepts you, likes you, loves you. His love has set you free. Follow His light into deeper relationships and more freedom than you've ever known before.

Read 1 John 4:16–21
Abba Father, may Your perfect love drive out all my fear.

When You Can...and Can't

He is my strength from day to day, without Him I would fall.
JESUS IS ALL THE WORLD TO ME by Will L. Thompson

Some days you just don't feel like you have the strength to go on. You're exhausted by a physical illness. Perhaps there's stress within your family. Work deadlines may be overwhelming. Or maybe a long list of dreaded tasks is dragging you down.

In any case, we all have days when we feel weak and long for help. We'd give anything for someone reliable to come along and walk beside us, lending strength and support to bring us through the day. To have such a friend can make the difference between pushing through and enduring, or just giving up.

Jesus is that Someone. He knows your vulnerabilities and weaknesses. He will give you strength when all you want to do is give up, and He holds you when you can no longer stand.

If you need strength for this day, lean on Him. He will not let you fall.

Read 2 Corinthians 12:10
Carry me through this time, Father, and give me strength for the days ahead.

New Creation

I give you my soul. I live for You alone.
I Give You My Heart by Reuben Morgan

It's an oxymoron, but Christians choose to give up free will. We relinquish control and surrender things like dreams and desires. Instead, we elect to submit to the Holy Spirit's instruction before committing ourselves to a course of action, knowing He is the biggest Dreamer of us all. In His hands, our lives will be far more useful than in our own.

The Gospel of Matthew tells us that "no man can serve two masters." As humans, we're familiar with that struggle. Temptations abound. But living for God alone requires us to relinquish those things that might detract from our wholehearted service to Christ.

The Bible calls this being "peculiar people." After giving our hearts to Christ, we begin to behave differently than the world does; we seek to love our enemies, pray for those who persecute us, turn the other cheek, keep the Ten Commandments, and leave revenge in God's hands.

Peculiar, indeed. However, it's a good deal, exchanging empty souls and worn-out hearts for life eternal with Jesus.

Read Philippians 1:21
I am Yours, Jesus, from the top of my head to the soles of my feet.

Unfamiliar Territory

Who can fathom the depth of Your love?
I Stand in Awe of You by Mark Altrogge

Nothing testifies to one's emotional frailties quite like getting married or having a child. The description of love given in 1 Corinthians 13 shines a spotlight on what love is supposed to look like.

Few of us can claim to be anything but a dim reflection of that example. The only infallible, unselfish love is the totally unfathomable love of God. It is radical, incomprehensible, irrational, and positively undeniable. Romans 8:38–39 assures us that nothing, no height or depth, angel, or any other created thing, absolutely nothing and no one can separate us from the love of God in Christ.

God loved us before we loved Him. His love cannot be measured by graph, meter, instrument, or equation other than John 3:16. God's love is pure, sacrificial, awe inspiring, and free to those who will accept it.

Before our first transgression, God already had a plan and a purpose to save us from the consequence of earthly life: sin and death. The name of that plan is Jesus.

Read Psalm 99:3
Father, I don't know why You love me, but I am so glad You do!

Cover Story

Nothing brings Him greater fame, when broken people call His name.
LIFT HIGH by Eddie Kirkland and Steve Fee

Have you heard a personal story that made your heart leap? Testimonies result from broken people giving witness to Christ's redemption in their lives. Woven within each one is a secondary miracle.

Blessed salvation is the primary miracle. Because of God's mercy, broken lives that could have ended in death and defeat are mended. And new believers are freed to share the good news of God's love and redeeming power with others.

The "secondary miracle" is what could have happened but didn't. Perhaps it's that you weren't overcome by depression when your spouse suddenly left or your child died; you didn't overdose on drugs; you didn't lose your home when you lost your job; you didn't abandon your faith when the cancer returned; you didn't perish in that house fire.

We all have miracles in our lives. Name yours. Announce the Lord's power!

Read Psalm 124
Lord, help me to remember to tell others about all the miracles in my life.

Devotion

I will serve You, give You everything.
You Are Worthy of Praise by David Ruis

The classic book *In His Steps* depicts one congregation's year-long challenge to live like Jesus. Without a doubt, God is worthy of our allegiance and complete obedience. But are we really serving Him in a sacrificial way?

Would we refuse to live with someone without a marriage covenant, even if it meant the loss of the relationship? Would we end friendships that ridicule our decision to live as Christians? Leave a job that forced us into unethical situations? God called Abraham to pack up his family and relocate. Would we?

The Word promises that whatever is given up in service to God will be returned a hundredfold along with eternal life (Matthew 19:29). Yet sacrifices are never convenient, and are often painful. Remember the cross?

Search your heart. Pray the Holy Spirit to enable you to wholeheartedly answer the Lord's call with "Here I am, send me!" No matter the cost.

Read Matthew 19:21–22
Lord, help me to never value anything more than I value You.

The Coming Kingdom

The kingdom of this world is become the kingdom of our Lord, and of His Christ.
HALLELUJAH CHORUS by George Frederick Handel

Kingdoms in this world come and go. World empires rise and fall. Kings, shahs, presidents, and emperors gain vast fame and power, only to disappear into the annals of history when their days are done. Sometimes the leaders rule well and the people are happy and prosperous. Others are cruel, bringing pain and devastation to their citizens. Still others, thirsting for power, lead their nations into battle. Property is stolen; hearts are broken; innocence dies.

All empires will eventually pale in comparison to the coming kingdom of our Lord. Since Jesus ascended into heaven, His people have been watching and waiting for the time of His return, when He will destroy the false rulers of this world. Though sin has corrupted our current condition, when Jesus comes again, this earthly domain will see its final hour and the kingdom of God will be established for eternity.

Will you be a citizen of that eternal kingdom? To whom do you swear allegiance this day?

Read Revelation 19:6
The promise of Your eternal kingdom keeps me going, Lord. Thank You.

Accessing God's Promises

For all that You've promised and all that You are, all that has carried me through.

Thank You, Lord by Dennis Jernigan

The word *promise* carries a lot of weight. Its synonyms are words like oath, guarantee, pledge, and vow—"binding" terms that are used in legal documents, partnerships, and long-term commitments. It only makes sense that we use such words, and enter into such agreements, with great care.

From Old Testament to New, we find God's promises throughout the Bible, intended for those who place their faith in Him as Lord of their lives. Do you want to know how to personalize His promises? Through thoughtful study and obedience to His Word. In the pages of your Bible is where He speaks His assurances to you. Assurances that He will hold you close through the trials and problems you face; that there is not a minute when He is not with you; that no matter how dire your situation, you can have confidence that God knows and cares. He has promised never to leave us. Our concerns are his.

God alone is able to see us through every problem.

Read Hebrews 10:23
How I love You and Your Word, God! Thank You for Your promises.

No Dice

Your Kingdom shall reign over all the earth!
Ancient of Days by Jamie Harvill and Gary Sadler

Benjamin Franklin once said, "In this world nothing can be said to be certain, except death and taxes." The quote has long been admired and repeated for its wit. Unfortunately, some people believe it's true. Cynicism, it seems, is contagious.

A more accurate observation was made by Albert Einstein: "God doesn't play dice." We may not be certain of many things, but we can have assurance of a few. God is not a gambler; He is faithful. His Word is unchanging. His long-awaited kingdom is definitely coming.

Because He is steadfast, our faith is not guesswork; our trust is not blind. It is more reliable to say God's kingdom will come than to say April 15 will come. For the believer, the promise of new life is even more certain than the inevitability of death.

His kingdom will come and reign forever. You can bank on it!

Read Lamentations 5:19
Father, the ways You fulfill Your Word make all the difference in this ever-changing world.

Going Home

When He comes, our glorious King, all His ransomed home to bring,
then anew this song we'll sing, hallelujah, what a Savior!
HALLELUJAH, WHAT A SAVIOR! by Philip P. Bliss

Heading off to college is an especially thrilling time for high school graduates—particularly if they are "going away" to school. The thought of independence and launching into adulthood is understandably exciting. Yet for many, after a few weeks of being far from the familiarity of family and friends, homesickness sets in. Suddenly the countdown to parents' weekend or Thanksgiving break begins. What a sweet meeting that first visit is! Conversation, laughter, and hugs abound.

Now, imagine the remarkable reunion we'll experience when Jesus returns to gather us, His children. It's a journey home so extraordinary that all God's people will erupt in praise and worship. Are you anxiously awaiting Christ's arrival? When Jesus comes back to gather His children, we will be filled with joy that demands a song.

Read 1 Thessalonians 4:16–17
Thank You for the hope of going home, Father.

Thirsty

I came to Jesus, and I drank of that life-giving stream;
my thirst was quenched, my soul revived, and now I live in Him.

I Heard the Voice of Jesus Say by Horatius Bonar

Water. When we're parched, we can think of nothing else. Quenching our thirst becomes vital. We can go for several days without food, but our bodies cannot survive for long without water. Our mouths dry out and our bodies feel like wrung-out sponges. In that state, given the choice between a pile of gold and a tall bottle of water, every one of us would choose the water.

Spiritual thirst is far worse than physical thirst. We strive to fill ourselves from sources we think can satiate our thirst—possessions, people, empty promises. But only Jesus can provide the life-giving stream that quenches a soul's thirst. He is the Living Water, never ending, ever flowing.

If you're feeling dried out, rung out, and thirsty, remember that Jesus supplies living water that quenches your deepest need.

Read John 4:13–14
Pour Your living water into my life, Jesus. Revive me.

Uninhibited Praise—Evermore!

To Thee, great One in Three, the highest praises be, hence evermore!
COME THOU ALMIGHTY KING, author unknown

The Duke of Wellington, the British military leader who defeated Napoleon at Waterloo, was a difficult man to serve. He was brilliant, demanding, and not one to shower his subordinates with compliments. Yet even Wellington realized that his methods left something to be desired. In his old age, a young lady asked him what, if anything, he would do differently if he had his life to live over again. Wellington thought for a moment, then replied, "I'd give more praise."

Why do we often find it difficult to give praise? For many of us, pride gets in the way. Even praising God may be difficult, since we're humbling ourselves; praise is equal to admitting that we don't deserve the credit for our successes or blessings.

Consider your life today; who sustains and secures you? Where does your hope come from? And have you thanked the One from whom all blessings flow?

Read Daniel 7:22
Father, Your forgiveness deserves all my praise.

Reaching for the Summit

I want to scale the utmost height and catch a gleam of glory bright.
But still I'll pray, 'til heaven I've found, "Lord, lead me on to higher ground."
HIGHER GROUND by Johnson Oatman, Jr.

The tallest mountain in North America—Mount McKinley in Alaska—towers 20,320 feet above sea level. Prior to the first summit ascent in 1913, several people falsely reported that they'd made it to the top, including one group of inexperienced climbers. People were so eager to be first, they were willing to lie about their efforts.

In our attempts to reach higher ground, we allow things like pride and jealousy to creep in and take the place of honor and integrity. We wish to climb other people's "mountains," rather than climbing the ones that God has placed before us. Whatever our mountain might be, it's essential to remember to let the Lord be our guide and to push for His glory, not our own. Only He can truly lead us to higher ground.

What mountain are you climbing today? Let the Lord lead. For He's leading you to higher ground in more ways than one.

Read Psalm 61:2
Thank You, Father, for climbing my mountains with me.

The Eye of the Storm

Whatever my lot, Thou hast taught me to say, "It is well; it is well with my soul."
It Is Well with My Soul by Horatio G. Spafford

How often do we long for God to show us what His plan is for our lives because we've grown tired of waiting, worrying, and wondering? If we're honest, we admit we crave more information because it gives us a measure of control and security.

For this reason we can be thankful for the testimony of Deuteronomy 31. In that chapter we're reminded through Moses that we have a God who goes before us; He will never leave or forsake us. Because of this, we don't have to worry or be afraid. Job loss, family stress, and financial struggles don't surprise our Lord.

Even when our path seems to peter out, circumstances blindside us, or we feel alone, we can rest assured that God hasn't abandoned us. We can claim His promise and know His comforting presence. Therefore, no matter what comes your way, you can say, "It is well with my soul," and trust that He has a plan for you.

Read Psalm 49:15
O keeper of my soul, help me to remember You are always with me.

So Tender

Love in that story so tender clearer than ever I see. Lord,
may I always remember love paid the ransom for me.

TELL ME THE STORY OF JESUS by Fanny J. Crosby

Can you imagine sacrificing your life for another human being? Many people claim they would give up their life for a child or spouse—but what about a stranger? Or worse yet, that person who has offended you, the one who annoys you or has hurt someone you love? Would you die for them too?

The story of the heavenly Father sacrificing His own Son has fascinated humanity and drawn people to God for the last two thousand years. In John 12, Jesus promised that if we would lift Him up, all men would follow. We can exalt Him by telling His story to our lost and dying world—by "going and making disciples." It's when the story of Jesus is proclaimed that searching souls are drawn to the cross and come face-to-face with a love beyond all measure.

Read Luke 24:32
I long to tell Your story to a lost and dying world.

A Royal Invitation

Welcomed in to the courts of the king.
FACEDOWN by Matt Redman

British Royal weddings are a spectacular sight. Thanks to modern media, we're given the chance to watch as commoners line the streets to catch a glimpse of the motorcade, look on while heads of state from around the world are escorted to honored seats, and see the newly married nobles kiss for the first time on the balcony of Buckingham Palace.

The likelihood of any average citizen being invited to a royal dinner with the queen is next to impossible. However, that's exactly what Jesus has done for us. As our Redeemer, He doesn't just give us access to heaven. Instead we are welcomed—like family—into His presence. With Him, there are no commoners, no "average" guests. We have been sought out, our presence specially requested. We are sons and daughters of the King!

Read Psalm 117:1-2
Lord, thank You for giving us access to You—our Prince of Peace.

The Morning Comes

Mourning turns to songs of praise.
Our God Saves by Paul Baloche and Brenton Brown

Traditionally, when sharing the gospel with someone who doesn't know Christ, we walk them through the book of Romans, explaining that the result of our sinfulness is eternal separation from Him—death. That same passage, however, goes on to say that the gift of God is eternal life.

Because of Jesus's victory over sin and the grave, we no longer have to fear or grieve death. Instead we can celebrate and enjoy the salvation provided by the sacrifice of our Savior, the Prince of Peace. This truth doesn't change the fact that we are destined to face physical death, but it changes everything to do with our perspective about it.

No longer does death have the final say. Because of Christ, there is life!

Read Matthew 28:19
Lord, thank You for the opportunity to be united with You.

The Conquering Symbol

I will cling to the old rugged cross, and exchange it some day for a crown.
THE OLD RUGGED CROSS by George Bennard

In ancient Rome, the cross was a symbol of suffering and shame. To be crucified was considered a death associated with the greatest guilt and curse. Today we see the cross as a symbol of God's infinite love for His people. We wear it as jewelry around our necks, tattoo it on our arms, and hang it as décor in our homes.

Jesus didn't deserve the cross and its humiliation, yet He chose to die and pay our sin penalty in full. This is love in its highest form. Love in its greatest capacity. Jesus knew that we were utterly helpless against sin and the power of death, so He chose to suffer and die in our place and conquer evil once and for all. Thanks to Him, death's most terrible instrument has become a soaring symbol of life eternal.

Read Hebrews 12:2
Help me never to forget the price You paid for my salvation.

By His Voice

We are His flock, He doth us feed, and for His sheep He doth us take.
ALL PEOPLE THAT ON EARTH DO DWELL by William Kethe

Sheep are pretty good listeners. As a shepherd spends time with his sheep, the whole flock begins to recognize his voice. They learn to trust and follow him, realizing he leads them, day by day, to tender grass in lush, green meadows. He protects them from predators, even sleeping at the mouth of the gate to keep them safe at night. He watches each and every one, noticing if any of them goes missing. There is such a connection between sheep and shepherd—such a deep form of trust and relationship—that a stranger cannot step into the shepherd's role. The sheep will ignore him.

Like sheep, we are created to listen for and know the voice of our Shepherd. The more time we spend with Him, the more we will grow to trust and follow Him. If we know His voice, we can distinguish it from those who are trying to mislead us.

Listen quietly in this moment for your Shepherd's voice. Then, follow.

Read Psalm 23
Father, help me to recognize the voice of my Shepherd.

Powerful Love

I see the stars, I hear the rolling thunder, Thy power throughout the universe displayed.
HOW GREAT THOU ART by Stuart K. Hine

Our universe is incredible, full of thousands of galaxies, whirlpools of energy, and matter. Our own galaxy exists like a perfect oasis within the vast cosmic mystery. Our earth is just one tiny part of it.

God is the all-knowing Creator of the universe. When there was nothing but darkness, God's power transformed it all into a perfect tapestry of stars, lights, water, and life. He hung the stars, moons, and planets. He designed the land to border the sea, and rivers and lakes to flow through the land.

Nothing was possible without God's miraculous power and plans.

God is truly great; He is miraculous and omnipotent. Take a moment and consider His greatness. His beauty. His power as the Author of all. Then remember that He created you as well.

Read Deuteronomy 10:17
Dear Lord, I worship You as the magnificent Creator of all.

Praiseworthy

Thou didst accept their praises—accept the praise we bring,
who in all good delightest, Thou good and gracious King!
ALL GLORY, LAUD, AND HONOR by Theodulph of Orleans

When we really think about it, we have little control or command over much that impacts us. Health and weather are ideal examples. We hear from friends that life was moving along "normally" until everything took an unexpected turn.

We see it on the news. It's at these times that we're reminded of our dependence on a mighty God who gives us everything we need for life—both now and for eternity. Though we're undeserving, He continues to graciously give.

Once we realize that the King of kings is the source of our life, health, and strength, we are compelled to praise Him. Though He allows us to take pleasure in the "stuff" of life such as accomplishments, possessions, and relationships, nothing and no one can compare to God.

Despite our limited view, in His greatness, God accepts our praise. He is our provider and sustainer. How will you praise Him today?

Read John 12:13
Dear God, help me to praise You with my lips—and with my whole life—today.

The Shepherd's Will

Early let us seek Thy favor; early let us do Thy will.
SAVIOR, LIKE A SHEPHERD LEAD US by Dorothy A. Thrupp

"If everyone else jumped off a cliff, would you do it too?" Rare is the parent who hasn't posed that question to their child at some point. As parents, we challenge our children not to give in to the influence or pressure from friends and peers—understanding that the struggle to follow the norm is one they'll face throughout life. While popularity and acceptance attract us, it is God's approval that matters.

Following the examples of others often puts us in difficult and potentially dangerous situations. Like sheep that will blindly follow one another off a cliff, we tend to imitate those around us, especially under pressure. For this reason, it is essential that we set out each day seeking our Father's plan and approval—following the Shepherd rather than our fellow sheep.

Today, seek His will and favor.

Read John 10:4–5
Good Shepherd, teach me to desire Your will and approval above all else.

Connected to Jesus

I'm alive because I'm alive in You.
ALL BECAUSE OF JESUS by Steve Fee

Strong storm winds of spring and powerful gusts of hurricanes often cause tree branches to crack. Limbs often succumb to the pressure, breaking away and blowing across nearby fields. Several branches, however, will stay connected. Some limbs may be large and ancient, and others more recent growth, yet both survive the winds and thus live on.

When the winds of life come against us, how strong will you be? Are you well nourished, so deeply connected to Jesus that no storm can tear you away? Or are you maintaining only a surface-level connection in hopes that it will be enough to sustain you? If the winds get too strong, will a crack form? Worse yet, will you become disconnected from Jesus—the true Vine—and wither into uselessness?

Our lives are best lived in strong connection to Him. We live because He lives in us.

How strong is your connection?

Read John 15:5–7
Jesus, teach me to live in You.

Life Metaphors

As I stumble in the darkness, I will call Your name by night.
GOD OF WONDERS by Marc Byrd and Steve Hindalong

Have you ever felt like you were in the dark when it comes to figuring out what life is about? Most of us do at some point, and our metaphors reflect that. People call life a puzzle, a roller coaster, a symphony, a lonesome highway. Other say it's a game of cards in which you have to play the hand you're dealt. Perhaps Forrest Gump summed it up best: "Life is like a box of chocolates; you never know what you're going to get."

It seems there are as many metaphors for life as there are people.

Scripture has its own metaphors. Life is chaff in the wind. An investment given to a servant by his master. A test. The Bible affirms life is short, difficult, and unpredictable. But it also affirms God loves us, and He cares how we live. We may struggle to figure out what life really means, but when we call on God's name in the night, He hears and will send His light.

Read Psalm 37:23–24
Lord, help me to live in the light of Your Word.

Dethroning Our Kings

King of my life, I crown Thee now. Thine shall the glory be.
Lead Me to Calvary by Jennie Evelyn Hussey

We may not realize it, but most of us want to rule like royalty over our lives. In other words, we expect to dictate what's going to happen and when. We set the agenda and stubbornly chase what we want to do today, tomorrow, next week, next year.

While it is good for us to make plans and set goals, we should hold onto them loosely, always realizing that the Prince of Peace wants to lead, guide, and direct. Our lives, after all, are not our own.

We find peace when we dethrone ourselves, release control, and put Jesus in His rightful role as King of our lives, trusting Him to lovingly guide and walk us into our futures. When we remove our own crowns and offer them to the rightful Heir to the throne, our lives will bring Him glory.

Have you crowned Jesus King of your life?

Read James 4:13–15
Lord, rule over my life, from the big goals to the details ahead of me.

Your Flickering Light

O Light that foll'west all my way, I yield my flick'ring torch to Thee.

O Love That Will Not Let Me Go by Cecil F. Alexander

In 1898, Conrad Hubert invented the flashlight. When the contraption was turned on, however, the light lasted only a few seconds. Gradually, additional experiments helped scientists understand that this light had to be connected to a power source—a battery—to create a continuous beam. Now, we even have flashlights with beams that can be used to point out stars.

New Christians often function like that first flashlight that shined brightly but only for a few seconds. Yet as we grow in our knowledge of God's Word and draw nearer to Him, our light shines brighter and longer. The trick is to yield our flickering light to God, our never-ending source of power. He uses our light to point the way for those who are lost.

Is your light flickering today? Make sure you're connected to the Light of the world.

Read Psalm 118:27

Father, I give You my life. May it shine brighter each day.

Our Journey's End

At the name of Jesus bowing when in heaven we shall meet.
King of kings we'll gladly crown Him when our journey is complete.

Take the Name of Jesus with You by Lydia Baxter

Step by step, year by year, we make our way through the days of our life, along high mountain ridges and through deep, dark valleys. Sometimes the path is sure, and other times it's rocky and treacherous. Yet always God's children can press on—moving forward in confidence that at the finish line we will meet our Lord face-to-face.

Those who are not believers think that life's journey ends at death. They consider what they see and know of this life to be all there is. For believers, however, we can celebrate. Death is not final; in fact, the most glorious part of our journey is just beginning when we take our last breath on earth!

The next time you are confronted with the loss of one of God's own, don't get caught up in the world's thinking. Death doesn't have the final say. Our Redeemer does—the King of glory. And He is alive in heaven, waiting to share eternity with you.

Read Revelation 22:12–13
Thank You, Jesus, that death doesn't have the last word.

August 13

A Place of Refuge

The name of the Lord is a strong tower; the righteous run into it and they are saved.
BLESSED BE THE NAME OF THE LORD (A STRONG TOWER) by Clinton Utterbach

April 11, 1965, is a day carved into the memory of anyone who lived through it. On that Palm Sunday, killer tornadoes ripped through numerous counties in Michigan, Indiana, and Ohio, leaving devastation in their wake. While many people lost their lives, countless others were saved by taking refuge in a basement or concrete shelter.

The name of our Lord is also a haven, a place to run when the "tornadoes" of life swirl around us, threatening destruction. The name of the Lord is a place of safety,

a place of salvation—steady, stalwart, solid. When we run to Him for shelter, He gives us peace. He wraps His arms around us, letting us know we are loved and treasured, protected from harm.

When you need a place of safety, head for your Strong Tower. There you will be sheltered from the storm. Safe and secure.

Read Psalm 61:3
Jesus, You are my place of refuge and strength.

God's Perfect Love

Living, He loved me! Dying, He saved me! Buried, He carried my sins far away! Rising, He justified freely forever! One day He's coming—O glorious day!
ONE DAY by J. Wilbur Chapman

It's easy to love someone who is perfect. But God demonstrated His love for us when we were imperfect by sending His only Son to save us.

We were turned in the wrong direction—away from Him and His will. Jesus turned us around and rescued us so that we could be at peace with Him and His Father. His desire was not only for our salvation but for our justification—so that an unholy people could be made right and stand before a just and holy God.

Praise Him! When our life on earth ends, we'll fall to our knees before God, but our Redeemer will gently help us to our feet. Because of Jesus, we will one day see God's face, because the Way has made a way.

Read Romans 5:6
Father God, You loved us enough to give Your Son. Amazing!

I'll See You There

He rose a victor from the dark domain, and He lives forever with His saints to reign.
CHRIST AROSE by Robert Lowry

All of us will eventually encounter the death of a loved one. Whether it is a beloved grandparent who has lived a long and full life or a friend gone too soon, we often don't understand the intensity of grief until we've experienced its coldness and shadows ourselves.

Though the length of anyone's journey on this earth is unsure, death is inevitable. That much we know. Still, the details of death's domain are shrouded in mystery. It's a mystery that makes many of us feel afraid and uncertain.

Yet one person did come back from death—our Lord Himself—and in the process overcame it forever. The Lord of life was dead and buried but rose victorious, and because He conquered death, we too will rise and reign with Him.

There is no need for fear! The victory is won when we trust in our living Savior!

Read 1 Corinthians 15:20–28
Jesus, thank You for the hope we have in You.

The Joyful Debtor

Come ye needy weary, heavy laden, lost and ruined by the fall.
Come, Ye Sinners by Joseph Hart

There are few things more depressing than debt. It burdens people with feelings of regret and inadequacy, causing them to feel overwhelmed and hopeless. It weighs on their minds and cripples their spirits. And it isolates them. How many people who are struggling with their finances feel comfortable proclaiming it to their closest friends and relatives? Not many. They are far more likely to fear judgment, and so they withdraw. And in the end, they feel more alone than ever.

Sin is similar to debt. It weighs on the wings of our souls, dragging us down even into depression. Fortunately, we can call on Christ. When we come to Him and confess our sins, He releases the weights from our shoulders. Christ died on the cross to pay all of our debts with His blood. He continually beckons us to dwell in His love and accept this gift He has freely given. The greater our debt, the greater joy we will experience when we are set free.

Read Luke 7:44–47
I cannot thank You enough for paying my debts, Jesus. That is a freedom worth proclaiming!

Come as You Are

I want to walk in a manner that's worthy of the gospel.

Your Grace by Andy Park

Walking in a manner worthy of the gospel requires dependence on Jesus; it has little to do with what we feel we're capable of on our own. We can never clean up enough to be good enough for salvation.

In Judges 6, the Lord reassured a doubtful Gideon to go on in the strength he had and let God do the rest. That's His promise to us too—to provide whatever is required as we step out in faith to live in a way that will bring Him glory.

The Holy Spirit will guide, convict, protect, and grow us as we submit to a relationship with Him; God's grace and mercy will triumph over our shortcomings.

Read Ephesians 1:4–7

Abba, You could have given up on me but You didn't. You waited. Thank You.

A Timeless and Immortal God

Before the hills in order stood or earth received her frame,
from everlasting Thou art God, to endless years the same.
O God Our Help in Ages Past by Isaac Watts

Life. Some call it a rat race, others refer to it as a vapor. Whatever the case, the truth is, it quickly passes by. From one week to the next, most of us endeavor to get ahead, accomplish key goals, or at the least keep our heads above water.

God, however, is timeless and immortal. He has no beginning or end. He was the same yesterday, just as He is today and will be tomorrow. Our heavenly Father is not bound to any scientific facts or theories. He is and always will be. He is the Creator and we are His handiwork. Isn't it interesting how God doesn't need us, yet our lives depend totally on Him? Every second of our lives is at His discretion. He controls every molecule of air we take in and every beat of our hearts.

How marvelous to know that He chooses that we live at this very moment—and that He wants to use us to accomplish His will. Let this knowledge encourage you to wisely use the time He so lovingly gives you.

Read Psalm 90
I thank You for every waking moment of the day, Lord. Your grace and mercy toward me are truly wonderful.

Living Lavishly

Thy bountiful care what tongue can recite? It breathes in the air; it shines in the light.
O Worship the King by Robert Grant

One friend was overheard telling a struggling companion: "The Word says even if you make your bed in hell, God's still with you there. There's nowhere you can go to get away from Him!" He meant it, of course, not as a threat but as a comfort. The truth is that the nurturing character of our heavenly Father is ever present. He watches over us no matter how far we wander from Him. And even when we feel like He is distant, He is there.

He knows how many minutes of sleep you missed last night. He counts the tears you've shed. He's aware of the cares weighing on your heart. It would take a whole book to detail the multitude of ways God cares for us.

Are your circumstances causing you to feel isolated and confused? Look for Him. He will bring light and life into every situation so you can testify to His overwhelming love. Choose to trust that out of His abundant concern for you, He is your haven. The King of the universe is for you—who can be against you?

Read Psalm 104:1
Today we will rest in Your watchful care, dear Father.

Common Denominator

Hallelujah, all my stains are washed away, washed away.
GRACE LIKE RAIN by Todd Agnew, Chris Collins, Edwin O. Excell, and John Newton

You may have experienced a myriad of feelings upon accepting Christ as your personal Savior. The heavy barrier of sin was lifted, and the Holy Spirit set to work immediately—infusing new life, hope, and promise.

For some, earlier tears of doubt and fear were instantly replaced with sobs of joy. Even if their feet didn't move a step, their souls began dancing. For others, accepting Christ may have come during quiet reflection. As their racing heart cried, "Yes, Lord!" the tenderness of God's love brought tears of silent joy to eyes still closed in prayer.

While everyone's conversion experience is different because each heart's journey to God is unique, there is one common denominator: grace. God's Word tells us that the heavenly realms rejoice each time a lost sheep returns home. Christ's sacrifice enables godly grace to fall down upon us all, washing away the stains of sin like warm rain falling from a summer sky.

Read Hebrews 9:12–14
Lord of heaven and earth, I praise You for this wondrous gift of eternal life.

The Victor

Broader than the scope of my transgressions, greater far than all my sin and shame;
O magnify the precious name of Jesus, praise His name!
WONDERFUL GRACE OF JESUS by Haldor Lillenas

Understanding the full scope of a military operation is absolutely necessary before even one soldier is deployed. A commanding officer must consider all threats to his troops, as well as the strategic advantages and the potential for victory. The ability to see the big picture increases the likelihood of triumph in each small segment of action.

Fortunately, as believers we know the battle for our souls has been won. Jesus, the Son of God, understood the threat of sin, waged war against the enemy, and rose victorious over sin and the grave. Death—both physical and spiritual—was defeated and we were redeemed, granting us the promise of eternal life.

Praise the prevailing Savior! Sound the trumpet and celebrate!

Read Ephesians 2:8–9
Thank You, conquering King, that because of Your grace, I am not condemned by sin.

Eternal Echoes

Still we are the voice in the desert, crying, "Prepare ye the way of the Lord!"
DAYS OF ELIJAH by Robin Mark

Eisenhower's interstate highway system is a grand accomplishment, but in terms of length it has yet to match the paved roads of the Roman Empire. In Jesus's time the adage "All roads lead to Rome" was quite true. At its peak, Rome had no fewer than twenty-nine military highways branching from the city. The roads covered most of the known world, spanning from England to Egypt.

The Roman Empire unwittingly prepared the way for Jesus. Similarly today, human endeavors are often self-serving, but God uses them for His purposes in the end. Every road we build should lead others to faith in Christ. Our work, whatever it may be, bears significance. If we stick close to the path of righteousness, we will prepare the way for others to follow.

Read Isaiah 40:3

I am humbled that You use my endeavors to bring glory to Yourself. Thank You, God.

Shield of the Spirit

What a refuge in sorrow! How the heart yearningly turns to his rest!
Under His Wings by William O. Cushing

Seven times throughout Psalms we read about taking refuge in the shadow of God's wings. In the New Testament, Jesus wept over Jerusalem, wishing that He could protect the people the same way a hen gathers her brood under her wings.

A bird's wings protect its young from predators—covering and camouflaging them until danger has passed. These feathery shields also serve as a shade from the sun and a warm haven from storms.

As children of God, we can take similar sanctuary under His wings. In times of grief and despair, our heavenly Father is tangibly present—a retreat for the beaten and weary. In life's storms He shields us from the enemy. And thankfully, throughout our day-to-day routine, He shelters us from the elements that can cause our hearts and wills to lag.

Read Psalm 91:4
I count on Your protection and rest, Father God.

Walking in Light

When we walk with the Lord in the light of His Word, what a glory He sheds on our way!
Trust and Obey by James H. Sammis

God instructs us in Matthew 5:48 to be perfect as He is perfect. The only way to come close to following this command is to learn how to discern His divine light in our lives. We do this by learning to search His Word diligently, trusting Him completely, and obeying Him explicitly.

The direction offered in the Bible should not be viewed as restrictions that hinder freedom but rather like street lamps showing us the way to go. God's Word, often referred to as a road map or guidebook, openly identifies places where the enemy lurks. Likewise, the Bible shines a light on our heavenly Father's immense love and how He's made a way for us to be overcomers—journeying to eternity with Him.

Jesus authoritatively states in John 14:6 that He is the Way, the Truth, and the Life. Everything that affects you also concerns God, both the seemingly minute and the monumental. You can confidently come to Him for guidance and instruction, and He will show you the path of life.

Read 1 Samuel 15:22

Jesus, I trust Your love for me is absolute.
Nothing You require will bring me harm.

Matchless

The prince of darkness grim, we tremble not for him—
his rage we can endure, for lo, his doom is sure. One little word shall fell him.

A MIGHTY FORTRESS IS OUR GOD by Martin Luther

If you were asked to name the opposite of happy, how would you respond? How about the opposite of slow? Or hot?

Now name the opposite of God in your mind.

Many of us would name Satan as God's opposite. God, however, has no equal opposition. Angel and man are both His creations. Satan cannot be the evil counterpart to the almighty heavenly Father. He never was, nor ever will be, God's equal. Our enemy's rages are actually sounds of his own defeat.

He knows that he has no authority to affect our salvation or eternity. His attacks initiate trials we must endure and temptations we must overcome, but in Christ, victory is assured.

God's power is limitless. His love is absolute and His authority is boundless.

Read Psalm 18:2

I am so grateful there is none like You, Lord Jesus.

Common Ground

She on earth hath union with God the Three in One,
and mystic sweet communion with those whose rest is won.
The Church's One Foundation by Samuel J. Stone

Throughout history, disagreements within the body of Christ have provoked church splits and spawned the formation of new denominations. Unfortunately, all too often these conflicts over nonessentials have caused God's people to lose sight of their purpose and trigger unchurched observers to question the point of Christianity in the first place.

Instead of dwelling on differences in our worship styles or teaching methods, consider the core tenets of God's Word that you can agree on. Despite our distinctions, it's more important to remember that as the representative church on earth, our one foundation is the Redeemer of all humankind—Jesus Christ. Together, our unified purpose is to be His hands and feet—sharing the gospel with the lost and welcoming them into the family of God for eternity.

All heaven rejoices when one comes into relationship with Jesus. Let us make certain we do not block their path.

Read 1 Corinthians 3:10–11
Jesus, help me not to be distracted by petty differences but to focus on caring for the lost.

Real Listening

Open our ears, Lord, and help us to listen.
Open Our Eyes, Lord by Robert Cull

The Shona people of Zimbabwe have a saying about what it means to really listen: "It went in the ear," they say, "and spread out its sleeping mat." How many times is that true of us when somebody gives us advice or simply tries to tell us about their day? It takes special attention and a conscious effort to allow what we hear to really sink in.

What about the way we listen to God? Listening to Him often demands some kind of action or change of attitude on our part. So when we open God's Word, and when we pray that our ears would be opened, we also need to ask that our hearts would be softened, that we would lay down our defenses and demolish any idols that may have taken God's place.

Only then will His Word be able to enter in and spread out its sleeping mat.

Read Matthew 13:15–16
Soften my heart, Lord, so I may listen better when You speak.

Divine Nourishment

Bread of heaven feed me till I want no more....
Strong Deliverer be Thou still my strength and shield.
Guide Me, O Thou Great Jehovah by William Williams

There's nothing like Mama's cooking in the familiar comfort of home. Just as our mouths water at the remembrance of favorite dishes, our souls hunger to spend time with our Father God, to linger at His dinner table for intimate conversation and deep companionship.

Why do we try to satisfy our cravings for Him with inadequate replacements such as work, sex, drugs, or popularity? Why do we starve our spirits while we stuff our bodies and minds with junk food? Is it because we think our God is too busy keeping the world spinning and we don't want to bother Him, or that we're too boring or disappointing to merit His attention?

We couldn't be further from the truth. He's overjoyed to see us at the kitchen door. The table is set, and a feast of His Word is laid out that will satisfy and strengthen us like nothing else can.

Read Isaiah 58:11

Father God, I'm here at the table, ready and waiting, excited to hear what You have to tell me.

Run to Him

Broken, I run to You, for Your arms are open wide.
HUNGRY by Kathryn Scott

Some days we wish we could just stay in bed, pull the covers up, and hide from the world. We wonder why bad things happen, why evil exists, and if any good we do will ever make a difference.

This world has a way of dashing hopes, breaking down our dreams, and sometimes even destroying what we've worked so hard to build. Feeling broken isn't where anyone wants to be, yet we all face brokenness at some point in life. So how can we put the pieces back together?

In those moments when we find ourselves broken, we can run to God. He's the only one who understands us completely and, as Creator, knows how to put our pieces back together.

Run to Him. He's waiting for you, and His arms are open wide.

Read Hebrews 4:15
I'm broken, Lord. Please put the pieces back together and hold me tight.

Our Everything

Oh Lord my God, to you I give my everything; take all that I am.
LET THE PRAISES RING by Lincoln Brewster

Are we really capable of giving our "everything"? We have so many possessions, yet somehow, giving away money or things is often uncomfortable. What if we end up needing it later? And in response, we hold on to what we already have while continuing to collect more.

While there's certainly wisdom in preparation, we ought to hold on to our belongings loosely. Why? Because it's already all God's anyway. Surrendering our earthly security to God acknowledges His lordship of our lives. We honor Him when we willingly give of ourselves and our possessions, all the while recognizing our dependence on Him to meet our needs—whether they be spiritual, emotional, physical, social, or intellectual.

Beyond the "stuff," however, we must also be willing to give who we are. When we trust God with our very lives, our futures, our dreams, our desires, then we have truly given Him everything.

Are you ready to give God everything?

Read Luke 21:1–4
May I trust You completely so I can give my everything to You.

Lead Me On

Jesus, take my life and lead me on.
Lord, You Have My Heart by Martin Smith

For some Christians, the "salvation transaction" is both the beginning and the end of their experience with God. They understand that Jesus died and was raised for them, and this is good news, so they have "accepted Him." But this way of describing our affiliation to the Creator, Sustainer, and Redeemer of the entire created universe hardly does justice to His true Lordship.

New Testament believers were very different. They understood that Jesus came to give them life, yes, but they also knew that He would transform them—that they would become new creations. From the very first time He summoned His disciples to follow, it was more than an afternoon walk beside a lake; it was a turn in their entire life journey—outside and in.

Following Jesus means not just accepting what He has to offer but surrendering our redeemed lives to Him. Are you ready to follow Him wherever He leads?

Read John 21:15–22
Lord, my life is Yours. I'm right behind You; lead me where You will.

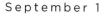

Safe Return

'Tis grace hath brought me safe thus far, and grace will lead me home.
AMAZING GRACE by John Newton

A young boy stood crying on the sidewalk outside a store, afraid because he'd temporarily gotten separated from his mother. The fear of being lost was immediate and overwhelming. Within seconds his mother appeared, equally terrified, and then—spotting him—relieved that her boy was safe.

Thankfully, we serve a God who safely guides us and never—not even for a moment—loses track of where we are. Every day we are safe because our heavenly Father cares for us. There's no need to fear anything or anyone. Because God's hands are holding us, there's no need to be concerned about the unknown; His grace gives us safety. We can have confidence that God will provide and care for us on this earth until the day we will be with Him forever.

On that final day, because of God's grace, Christ will lead the redeemed to our eternal home. What an ideal sense of security that provides!

Read Ephesians 2:8
Lord, thank You for my eternal home and safety with You.

Constant Companion

Precious Jesus, Savior, Friend; And I know that He is with me, He'll be with me to the end.
'Tis So Sweet to Trust in Jesus by Louisa M. R. Stead

Jesus has many names: Redeemer, Mediator, and Deliverer, to list a few. It's a remarkable gift to have a holy Ally with us every moment of every day.

God holds true to His promise to never leave nor forsake us. He is our ever-present help. As Friend, Jesus lovingly endures every situation in our lives and persists until we take our last breath. As Counselor, the Holy Spirit is never too busy or tired to listen to the concerns and joys of our hearts. As Savior, Christ has rescued us from the sins that threaten to enslave us. Nothing compares with the peace we achieve when we surrender our lives to His care.

His love will remain constant even as we step from our mortality to the glory of life everlasting. At the close of earthly life, already having prepared a place for us, Jesus will also welcome us home.

Read 1 Timothy 4:10
Jesus, how I love You because You first loved me.

Relentless Deliverance

Everyone needs compassion, love that's never failing. Let mercy fall on me.
Mighty to Save by Reuben Morgan and Ben Fielding

God's capacity to love the unlovable, pardon the unforgivable, and redeem what seems hopeless is beyond human understanding. When we ask Christ into our hearts, our sins are immediately absolved, our present comes under the Holy Spirit's direct guidance, and our eternal future in heaven is secured. In that same moment, God's compassion has given us more than we could ever think to ask for. Through Jesus, God's mercy now falls across our shoulders and covers us like a blanket. As we continue to walk in God's ways, He lovingly, mercifully, and unfailingly corrects our steps and fights our battles. By His might, truly no enemy can stand against us.

This is the God we serve: powerful over sin, amazing in grace, unfailing in love, endless in compassion, incomparable in mercy. There is no God like Jehovah!

Read Psalm 103:12
You gave me everything, Lord, when You gave me You.

Claiming Our Inheritance

Joint heirs with Jesus as we travel this sod.
THE FAMILY OF GOD by Gloria Gaither and William Gaither

In the legal world, an heir is someone who has the right of inheritance. We speak of the child of a king as being an "heir apparent," or someone who should, by legal right, inherit the throne. Because of Jesus's redemptive work on the cross, believers have been made heirs of the Most High God. We have become God's beloved sons and daughters of the King of kings. As joint heirs with Jesus, everything that God has for Jesus is for us too. In the same way that God loved Jesus, He loves us.

The same strength that God provided for Jesus has been given to us. The many blessings He poured out on Jesus He pours out on us.

Are you ready to claim your inheritance? Then do as Jesus did: obey your Father's will.

Look for ways today to reflect Him today.

Read 1 Corinthians 12:13
I long for others to see You through me, Father.

Lead Me, Lord

I want to follow Jesus.
I Want to Walk as a Child of the Light by Kathleen Armstrong Thomerson

Follow the leader. Whether we're in Boy Scouts, the military, or employees in a company, we look to our leader to show the way. Our part is to learn to heed that person's direction, because the truth is, a leader can lead to the ends of the earth, but he cannot force anyone to follow.

In our Christian walk, willingness is key. God won't force us to follow Him, and He won't drag us onto paths of righteousness. His Spirit will gently fuel our appetite to be led but will never overpower our will.

Our desire to follow Jesus will increase as we grow in Christ. We can't go wrong when "I want to follow Jesus" is our heart's cry. God used fire by night and a cloud by day to show the Israelites where to go. Thankfully, He gave us an even greater witness: the Holy Spirit.

Read Ephesians 5:8
Jesus, I want to follow only You.

Overcoming

Lord renew my mind, as Your will unfolds in my life.
THE POWER OF YOUR LOVE by Geoff Bullock

Life's unexpected, unplanned circumstances can leave us breathless. Shocking situations come up that leave us feeling helpless—causing us to stagger from the impact. Sometimes we're stuck, unsure of how to get over, around, or through a crisis.

As believers, we can trust that our best recourse is to hold tightly to Jesus's hand while we wait for His perfect will to unfold. If we're open to it, God can use trials to bring spiritual renewal and redirection for us instead of devastation. Every precious moment spent in His Word and in prayer will help solidify that process of bringing us peace, affirmation, and guidance, while replenishing our joy in Christ.

God can supply just what we need to be restored. The power of His love for us means that He knows exactly what it will take for us to get through a trial and move on to life more abundant. Trust Him. He promises to guide and protect us all.

Read Romans 12:2
I don't have answers but You do, Lord. Please sustain and guide me.

Putting Feet to Our Faith

So send I you to bind the bruised and broken...to wake, to bear the burdens of a world aweary.

So Send I You by Margaret Clarkson

Most Christians are familiar with the Great Commission and its command to us to spread the gospel and make disciples. However, it's easy to think that evangelism is the job of "professional Christians" like pastors and clergy. Not so! Jesus's charge to each believer is to continue the king-dom-building work. The Great Commission is not a suggestion—it is a divine order! We are called to take the Good News outward, in ever-broadening circles; to comfort and bring hope to the fearful. We are God's instruments to spread the gospel.

Today's the day to intentionally put feet to our faith. Let's show the love and concern of our Savior to all we meet.

Read John 20:21
Show me how to serve Your people and love those You cherish.

The Perfect Pardon

The vilest offender who truly believes, that moment from Jesus a pardon receives.
To God Be the Glory by Fanny J. Crosby

The psalmist declared, "The Lord has done great things for us; and we are glad" (Psalm 126:3 NKJV). But the word glad hardly seems sufficient.

In the legal world, a pardon is the official act of forgiving a crime. It is an executive decree that can only be accomplished by a state governor or the president. With a pardon, the conviction is erased from the records and the person is freed from further punishment. In the life of the believer, our being born into sin made us criminals in the eyes of a just and holy God. Yet rather than letting us face the ultimate penalty for sin—death—God loved us so much that He sacrificed His Son to die in our place. When Jesus died on the cross, all of our sins, past, present, and future, were forgiven. We were pardoned and our record was cleared. Forever.

Read Psalm 126:3

For sending Your Son to die in my place, heavenly Father, I am overcome with thanks.

Trusting God in the Dark

Singing if my way is clear, praying if the path be drear.
Trusting Jesus by Edgar P. Stites

Waking up to a sunny, blue-sky morning on a Carolina beach is a dream vacation for many. But visit that same beach during a fierce storm, such as a hurricane, and it's frightening.

It's difficult to relax when the road ahead is unclear. When the storms of life swirl around us and circumstances seem turbulent, the future becomes ominous. Trusting God when facing the unknown calls for our faithful trust—for commitment. It's quite a loaded word, especially in our spiritual lives. But as we commit matters to God we can be free from the confusion, conflicts, and worries of our everyday lives.

There is no area of our lives that is beyond God's loving concern—our employment, our families, our friendships all matter to Him. Our heavenly Father will hear and answer our prayers.

Read Psalm 37:5
Lord, I trust You with every area of my life. I will seek Your will and Your way as I make my daily decisions.

Calling Your Name

Called by name into Your presence, undeserved, holy God.
LORD I COME by Geraldine Latty

Every year television brings the Academy Awards—the Oscars—into our homes. Nominees are announced in each category and the cameras shift to the nervous contenders anxiously waiting in the audience, the tension obvious in their faces. Will I win, they wonder, or will I just be an "also nominated" footnote?

Next, the presenter tears open the envelope, reads the contents, and calls out, "The Oscar goes to..." Suddenly the cameras focus on the winner as he or she hurries up to the stage to receive the award and bask in the glory of recognition.

God is calling your name. You don't have to wait in suspense to find out whether you can come into the glory of His presence. He has already chosen you and invited you—not because of your accomplishments, not because you deserve it, but just because He loves you.

Read Hebrews 10:19–23

I'm listening, Lord. Thank You for calling my name.

Gratefully Surrounded

Come into His presence with thanksgiving in your heart.
COME INTO HIS PRESENCE BY LYNN BAIRD

Jesus conquered sin and death. He turned mourning into dancing. To come into His holy presence is to know pure love and such joy that the heart is overwhelmed with gratitude.

Think of who you were in your sin and where you would be now if Jesus had not made a way for you to approach His throne of grace. There are no sufficient words to express our thanks for His mercy.

As He was one with the Father during His earthly ministry, so are we, as His disciples, one with Him through the continuing ministry of the Holy Spirit.

This is why, even during trials and hard times, we can be sure of His presence and thankful that Jesus is our constant source of living water that will never run dry. Happiness is fleeting, but life in Christ brings joy eternal.

Read Psalm 100:2
There is no need for the stones to cry out, God, for I will praise You!

What's in a Name?

Heaven and earth rejoice in His holy name.
HE IS EXALTED by Twila Paris

Parents toil over choosing the "right" name for their child. Should it be a traditional family name? A biblical one? Or perhaps one rife with meaning? After all, a strong name can provide direction and purpose.

Consider just a few of the names of Jesus: Son of God, Cornerstone, Savior, Redeemer, Messiah, Deliverer…. The list goes on and on. And yet, somehow, He perfectly fulfills each one. Truly the greatness of Christ demands the worship of every living being.

He satisfies our every need.

The Bible tells us that at the name of Jesus, every knee will bow and every tongue will confess that Jesus Christ is Lord. There will definitely be a day, and soon to come, when all will finally acknowledge Him as the Savior of the world. His name is holy.

Read Psalm 34:3
You are the true God that the whole world will one day exalt.

Be Glorified

In my life, Lord, be glorified.
LORD, BE GLORIFIED by Bob Kilpatrick

"It's not all about you." It's a statement that we might say with sarcasm to friends and family. But the truth is, it's not about us. As believers, our lives are not our own; as part of the body of Christ, we become the hands and feet of God. There we do well to ask ourselves, Do my actions reflect His heart?

John's Gospel tells us the story of Lazarus, who so sick that his sisters feared for his life and sent for Jesus to heal him. If there was ever a family who thought that it should all be about them—at least for a little while—it was Lazarus and his sisters. It's how we all feel when we're in the center of a crisis. However, Jesus responded, "This sickness will not end in death. No, it is for God's glory so that God's Son may be glorified through it."

The sickness did not end in death, but it began there. First came death, then resurrection from the dead. First came loss, sorrow, and weeping. Then came Jesus!

Despite our pain or humiliation, God will be glorified. He works through all things, good and bad.

Read John 11
Be glorified in all aspects of my life, great God.

Sing!

Stand and sing to broken hearts who can know the healing power of our awesome King of love.
SHOUT TO THE NORTH by Martin Smith

Children love singing. Lullabies soothe them and funny tunes make them laugh. They revel in learning easy-to-remember melodies.

As we grow up, we never quite lose that love—or need—for music. The "soundtrack" of our lives gets formed, and on it are songs that we identify with specific occasions and years, good and bad. Sometimes our pain is so great that only music can bring us comfort. But it is worship songs especially that seem to connect God's weary and grieving children with Him.

Aren't you glad that the healing power of God works whether we can hold a tune or not? Its power isn't diminished or enhanced in the least by our musical ability. So don't hold back; sing to God! Make a joyful noise! And count on the Spirit to use the right song to bring healing—for you and for others.

Read Psalm 81:1
Father, help me take in and share Your healing songs of praise.

Alpha and Omega

He lives and grants me daily breath. He lives, and I shall conquer death.
I KNOW THAT MY REDEEMER LIVES by Samuel Medley

Take a minute to think about the ways in which God operates in and through you. Consider just the basics—each day He supplies us with everything it takes to live and move. Every breath we take is granted by the Master. What a testimony of His power and love.

In Genesis 2 we read that God breathed life into Adam and he became a living soul. And our Maker did the same for each of us. Astounding, isn't it? You are a phenomenal, unique creation. And because Jesus triumphed over death, all who believe in Him are living miracles destined for eternal life.

Now, take a deep breath and say thank You. Take another one, and imagine His mighty presence living inside you—the same Spirit-filled power that first gave man life and then conquered death, hell, and the grave.

Praise Almighty God, who was at the beginning and will be until the end.

Read Job 19:25

Creator and Redeemer, thank You for giving me life on earth and throughout eternity.

all about Him

I'm sorry Lord for the thing I've made it when it's all about You. It's all about You, Jesus.
THE HEART OF WORSHIP by Matt Redman

A popular line of posters, T-shirts, and cards features a self-centered bunny who proclaims, "It's all about me. Get used to it." While this may seem funny on the surface, the underlying meaning is clear: everything revolves around me. No one is more important than me!

Unfortunately, it's a common philosophy. We draw attention to ourselves, brag about our achievements, gloat over our plans. We forget that we only exist because of our Lord. Our very lives are dependent upon our Creator. How could we presume to think that everything exists to please us when we were created to please God? He provided us with talents, abilities, skills, and gifts that we are to use to glorify Him, not ourselves.

Above all, we were created to worship Him. When we focus on Him instead of ourselves, we worship as He desires. It's all about Him. Nothing else.

Read Hebrews 12:28
Help me to recognize that everything revolves around You, Jesus.

Assurance through God

Because He lives, I can face tomorrow.
BECAUSE HE LIVES by William J. and Gloria Gaither

Tomorrow. It's a word that carries both doubt and potential.

None of us know how long we will live, so thoughts of tomorrow make us feel uncertain. But our heavenly Father created our earthly bodies with an eternity of relationship in mind. While our mortal bodies will deteriorate and wear out, God's loving care daily renews our faith. As we rely on Him and trust in the promises contained in His Word, our faith increases.

With faith, we can weather tragedy, suffering, and death. The trials we face pale in comparison to the glorious hope we have in God through Jesus. And eventually we understand that what tomorrow brings is unimportant because we know Who brings tomorrow.

Read Philippians 3:10
Help me to look past my present situation, Lord, and into the glorious tomorrow with You.

Imagining Heaven

Will I sing "Hallelujah"? Will I be able to speak at all?
I Can Only Imagine by MercyMe

Many books have been written on the subject of heaven. The Bible gives us John's account of what heaven looks like in the book of Revelation, but even that is difficult to understand. How can anyone describe a place that defies all human understanding and experience? When we finally meet Jesus face-to-face, what will that be like?

We can only imagine how we will feel when we finally stand before our Savior. There will be a myriad of reactions to the Author and Finisher of our faith. Some will kneel while others will reach for His embrace. Some will sing "hallelujah!" and others will be speechless. Some will dance while others will sit quietly at His feet.

If we have accepted His gift of salvation, one day we will see Him face-to-face. We can only imagine what that day will be like, but we know it will be better than we can even fathom.

Read 2 Corinthians 5:8
Lord, I can't wait to see You! Thank You for making heaven possible for me!

Hunger

And nothing I desire compares with You.
MORE PRECIOUS THAN SILVER by Lynn DeShazo

Often during pregnancy an expectant mother will have specific, sometimes unusual, cravings. Depending on the woman and the time of day, she may hunger for anything from chocolate to pickles—or weird combinations of unusual foods. It's not uncommon for husbands to have to get out of their comfortable beds at odd hours to go in search of the only ingredient that will satisfy the soon-to-be momma. Once the baby is born, though, these cravings cease.

Much as an expectant mother experiences cravings, the people of God should hunger to be with Him, to long to know Him and experience His perfect peace. In *The Practice of the Presence of God*, Brother Lawrence wrote, "There is not in the world a kind of life more sweet and delightful than that of a continual conversation with God. Those only can comprehend it who practice and experience it." May our greatest desire be to fellowship with the Father.

Read Proverbs 8:11
May my desire for you never cease, God.

Supernatural Acts

Tell the world of His great love, our God is a God who saves.
Let God Arise by Chris Tomlin, Jesse Reeves, and Ed Cash

There is no challenge our God cannot meet and overcome. Chapter after chapter in the Bible alludes to miracles the Lord performed. He parted seas, restored lives, healed the sick, forgave adulterers, and cast out demons.

Some may think God is no longer in the miracle business, but He definitely is. He is no less God, no less powerful, and no less on-task today than He was in Bible times.

To find a miracle today, you won't have to look far—probably no further than family or friends. Almost everyone has heard about an unexplained, miraculous event. The secular world calls such incidents luck or coincidences, but as Christians, we recognize God's handiwork.

Next time you hear such a story, use it as a bridging opportunity to talk about Jesus with others. God not only has the compassionate love and willingness to grant unexpected blessings, He has the power to save.

Read 1 Timothy 1:14–16
Jesus, I know grace, mercy, and all good things come from You.

Do You Believe?

Sometimes I feel like shouting glory, glory, glory! Were you there when He rose up from the dead?
WERE YOU THERE? African-American Spiritual

Some stories seem far-fetched, don't they? Depending on the storyteller, we're likely to have an "I'll believe it when I see it" mentality. For many, the first testimony they hear about a heavenly Savior who came to earth to die and rise again seems a bit... sketchy.

It's true—the biblical resurrection story requires trust. It's only by faithful understanding, through the Holy Spirit, that we can believe it ever happened. But through this conviction in the resurrection, we can place faith in a risen Savior. Hebrews 11:6 (ESV) says, "Without faith it is impossible to please him, for whoever would draw near to God must believe that he exists and that he rewards those who seek him."

Just as it takes faith to believe that Jesus lived, it requires faith to believe that He rose from the dead. Even though we were not there in the flesh to see these events for ourselves, God gives us the ability to believe. Do you believe?

Read Mark 15:25

My dear Jesus, because of Your crucifixion, I am assured of one day meeting You face-to-face.

Both Feet

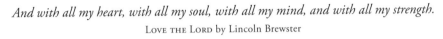

And with all my heart, with all my soul, with all my mind, and with all my strength.
LOVE THE LORD by Lincoln Brewster

A half tank of gas will often only take you partway to your destination if you're traveling a long distance. Eating merely a portion of your supper will leave you hungry. Taking just some of the doctor-prescribed medicine will keep you from experiencing complete healing.

In a similar way, it's too easy to fall into the trap of thinking we can surrender just a portion of our lives to God and keep some parts for ourselves. By agreeing to relinquish only partial control to Him, we are missing out on the full extent of the blessings He has for us.

It's important that we surrender every part of ourselves to the Lord. He is a jealous God, and He made clear His desire to Moses on Mount Sinai. God wrote, "You shall have no other gods before me" (Exodus 20:3 NIV).

God was saying, "I am not sharing." He wants all of us. Today is the day to give God our all.

Read Mark 12:30
Lord Jesus, today make my mind, body, soul, and spirit Yours.

What's in a Name?

He is the mighty King, Master of everything.

His Name Is Wonderful by Audrey Miei

The Bible lists over seven hundred names for Jesus: Lord, Mighty Counselor, Lamb of God, Messiah, Son of David, Redeemer, Savior, Bread of Life, and Alpha and Omega, to name a few. Have you ever wondered why there are so many? In biblical times, parents often named their children based on some descriptive aspect of their child's character or appearance. In Jesus's case, His many names served as a description of how He impacted the lives of those He touched. Matthew's Gospel opens by referring to Jesus as the "Son of David," which speaks to Jesus's lineage. In John 6:48, Jesus calls Himself "the Bread of Life," meaning that

He is the spiritual source that sustains us all.

One of the most powerful names for Jesus is Alpha and Omega—the first and last letters of the Greek alphabet. He is the omnipotent One! The first and the last, the Master of everything! He was the beginning and He will be the end!

Claim His name for your situation today. He promises to be everything you need!

Read Revelation 1:8
King of Glory, Savior of us all, Omnipotent One, thank You that in everything we can call on Your name!

Worthy

For all You've done and yet to do, with every breath I'm praising You.
FAMOUS ONE by Chris Tomlin and Jesse Reeves

Hollywood presents lifetime achievement awards to actors who have, over several decades, received significant acclaim for their work and won the hearts of millions of fans. During the ceremony, clips from their many movies are shown, and as the actor accepts the honor, admirers wonder what future projects lie ahead.

If celebrities can earn that kind of recognition, how much more does the one true God deserve our ultimate honor and praise? From the creation of the world, He has revealed His awesome power. Throughout history—in the lives of men and women—He has put His holiness and love, goodness and justice, might and grace on display. From Eve to Daniel, from Mary to the boy with the loaves and fishes, our incredible God has shown Himself worthy of all our acclaim. And He's not done yet! He continues today to accomplish His purposes.

Look to the future with expectation—He's there before you, preparing the way.

Read Psalm 107:22
Father, I am excited about the amazing work You want to accomplish through me.

Set Free

*I woke—the dungeon flamed with light! My chains fell off,
my heart was free, I rose, went forth, and followed Thee.*
AND CAN IT BE THAT I SHOULD GAIN? by Charles Wesley

We often use analogies such as "living in darkness" or "being in bondage to sin" to describe the spiritual condition of those who have not accepted Christ as their personal Savior. Only those who have received rescue from the dark prison of sin can understand what it means to be free in Christ.

When we have that "aha moment" and acknowledge Jesus as our Redeemer, when we realize that He desires a relationship with us—and that we need Him, truly need Him—our lives are instantly changed. It's as if we flipped a switch and the light shines in our lives for the first time. We see the ways in which our sins have held us captive, in the past and in the present. But as followers of Christ, we are no longer under the authority of sin but the authority of our Savior. Suddenly we are equipped to push old sin habits behind.

Do you know someone who needs to be free from sin's hold? Tell them about Jesus today.

Read 1 Thessalonians 5:9
Sovereign Lord, Your never-ending, always-abounding grace sets me free.

Time Flies

Be still my soul! The hour is hastening on when we shall be forever with the Lord.
BE STILL MY SOUL by Katharina von Schlegel

Remember when you couldn't wait to grow up? Eighteen seemed like the ultimate age; once you made it there, independence! Now you're an adult with mortgage payments, active children, looming debt, and career demands, wondering where the years went.

Instead of longing for your youth, savor today. Make time to appreciate what God has done and is yet to do. And learn to appreciate the challenges. Whether you're dealing with financial obligations, rebellious kids, or a difficult colleague, everything is designed to demonstrate God's love and mercy.

Yes, time moves quickly, but God has given you the gift of abundant life today, with the promise of eternity ahead. So be still, and trust that He is in control of the details, even as time marches onward.

Read Psalm 46:10
Teach me to be a good steward of every moment I have here on earth.

Released from Bondage

He breaks the power of canceled sin; He sets the prisoner free.
O For a Thousand Tongues to Sing by Charles Wesley

There's a story about a chicken whose foot was tied to a stake in the ground. Round and round the chicken ran, limited by its leash, only able to move two feet in any direction. One day, a kind stranger came along and cut the twine. Sadly, even though the chicken suddenly had the run of the barnyard, it continued to move in the same restricted circle.

Sometimes we exhibit chicken-like behavior, don't we? The moment we accepted the truth of Jesus's sacrifice, we were liberated from everything that had imprisoned us in a cycle of weakness. But at times we still struggle to embrace our new freedom, to stretch our boundaries and explore the new paths God has appointed for us. Occasionally we allow condemnation to sneak in and convince us that we really should punish ourselves for something we've done wrong, instead of confessing it and receiving forgiveness. By doing so, we act like chickens who don't know they're free.

Read Psalm 35:28
Don't let me squander the freedom You've granted me, Lord.

Bad to Blessing

Help me then in every tribulation, so to trust Thy promises, O Lord.
Day by Day by Lina Sandell

Bad days can be frustrating, but have you ever considered that your bad day may be...a blessing? You're already running late for work, and traffic is backed up because of a car accident. Could that have been you if you'd arrived at the intersection ten minutes earlier?

Life throws such circumstances our way every day. Circumstances that seem poorly timed and oh-so-inconvenient. And yet what we don't see are the "almosts" that God has shielded us from.

The Bible doesn't say "if" trouble comes; it says "when" trouble comes. So, while bad days are guaranteed, we can be thankful: God is able to use bad days to bless us. We can trust Him in them, even if we can't see the blessing beyond the difficulty.

Read Psalm 20:1
Remind me to look for today's blessings in disguise, Lord.

No Hands, Only Him

Fear not, I am with thee; O be not dismayed, for I am thy God, and will still give thee aid.
How Firm a Foundation, author unknown

Learning to ride a bicycle can be scary. The fear of falling, as well as the pain and embarrassment that go along with it, intimidates children. Some parents try to counter this by attaching training wheels; others run alongside their child until they're comfortably "cruising." Ultimately, we want our kids to be assured that they're not alone—that we're right beside them, supporting them.

Likewise, our heavenly Father assures us that we can trust in His presence and protection, that we need not fear what may come, because He will never leave His children.

Read 2 Thessalonians 2:13–17
Lord, help us to stand with confidence in You!

Rescued!

O the sound of salvation come, the sound of rescued ones.
O Praise Him (All This for a King) by David Crowder

The closer we are to defeat, the more welcome the saving reinforcements; the nearer we are to death, the more dramatic the rescue.

God's Word reads like a thrilling rescue. A man and his family find themselves afloat in an ark with two of every kind of animal in the midst of a worldwide flood. The only things standing between mankind and extinction are wooden boards and tar—and, of course, God's protection.

The Israelite nation trembles in fear as they realize they stand trapped between Pharaoh's army and the Red Sea, then God opens a way through the waters, saving His people and crushing their pursuers.

The most dramatic rescue stories are still being written today in the hearts of those who realize their desperate state and call out to Christ. "You see, at just the right time, when we were still powerless, Christ died for the ungodly" (Romans 5:6 NIV).

Today, join the chorus of rescued ones!

Read Colossians 1:12–14
Father, with my life I want to say thank You for rescuing me from darkness.

The Call

Rescue the perishing, duty demands it—strength for your labor the Lord will provide.
RESCUE THE PERISHING by Fanny J. Crosby

Soldiers and other public servants such as firefighters and police officers have an incredible sense of duty. Trained and equipped, they sacrificially take on the welfare of others as their personal responsibility. So should it be with those of us whose eternal life is secure in Jesus.

No matter which way we turn or where we look, there are people around us who are perishing. Physically. Emotionally. Spiritually. The needs are insurmountable. Nonetheless, in humility, we are reminded that God created us to be His hands, feet, and mouth here on earth. While we cannot fulfill the enormous task to rescue the perishing in our own strength, in Christ we can do all things (Philippians 4:13). God will provide the strength necessary to fulfill the assignment He has graciously given.

Activate your faith today, and extend hope to those who need rescue.

Read Jude 1:23
God, prepare me as a vessel to rescue the lost.

The Shortness of Life

Life is but a fleeting breath, a sigh too brief to measure.
PSALM 62 by Stuart Townend and Aaron Keyes

The world offers three basic reactions to the brevity of life. Denial is one, but death is much too common and hits too close to home to allow us to deny its presence for long.

Despair is another reaction, choosing to move through this short life under a cloud of depression and anxiety, waiting for the inevitable. A third option is to simply live for the moment—do what feels good regardless of the consequences. We may die tomorrow, so let's live it up today!

God offers us another alternative—to live for Christ now, in this short time on earth, because one day we will have eternity with Him. What a difference this truth makes in our outlook on life and death! It enables us to live joyfully in the moment, while urging us to live faithfully for the future.

Praise God!

Read 1 Corinthians 15:54–58
Jesus, You filled my life with meaning and purpose! What a wonderful gift!

Our God and King

There is a King that we adore, with humble hearts we bow before You, Lord.
GLORIOUS by Chris Tomlin and Jesse Reeves

We believers adore our King. It goes beyond a ruler-and-his-subjects relationship. We bow in awe of Him. God's magnificence is a reflection of His unbelievable beauty, power, righteousness, and perfection. As believers, we are the grateful recipients of His holiness, His goodness, and His love. Our adoration of God is a result of our understanding that He created us to display His glory. Despite our failures. Despite the sacrifices it took to redeem us.

Each day we have the blessed opportunity to emulate His character—reflecting His grace and love to a dying world as we care for others. We show Him our gratitude when we look beyond the faults of others and selflessly address their needs. We humbly acknowledge and bow down before our King when we share the gospel of Jesus Christ with men and women who, like us, would be lost without it.

Read Isaiah 43:7
Heavenly Father, Your mercy is demonstrated to me day after day.

Evidence

From the highest of heights to the depths of the sea Creation's revealing Your majesty.
Indescribable by Laura Story

God is wonderful; nature's variety is a testimony to Him. If you ever get the opportunity, take a road trip. God's created wonders will begin to unfold and reveal His majesty as you leave urban sprawl behind.

Rediscover awe as you view mountains—standing just the way they did when God carved them. Your lungs will delight in smog-free skies and your eyes will marvel at cobalt-blue lakes glittering in the reflected sun. Plan to stop frequently. Emerald forests offer nature trails delightful to the nose and eyes, and campsites near crystalline rivers that ripple with fish in season. Glancing across the vastness of cresting ocean waves or waving wheat fields imparts the true meaning of "as far as the eye can see."

From immense forests and rolling hills to stark deserts and sunsets splashed with crimson, fuchsia, gold, and sapphire, everything God created sparkles with His love and reveals His majesty.

Read Psalm 93
Creator, the world bears Your imprint, and my heart marvels at all You have made.

Embraced

Red and yellow, black and white, they are precious in His sight.
JESUS LOVES THE LITTLE CHILDREN by Clare Herbert Woolston

Energetic, loving, curious, honest, funny, smart...all these are words that describe the nature of children. With unconditional love, a child smiles and lights up the room. With pure hearts and innocence, children naturally desire to learn about and understand this amazing world. Every moment is an opportunity for them to grow as they approach new situations with curiosity and enthusiasm.

Jesus warmly welcomed the children. As a matter of fact, He scolded His disciples for trying to send them away. He utilized them as examples for all of us: "Truly I tell you, anyone who will not receive the kingdom of God like a little child will never enter it" (Mark 10:15 NIV).

God is pleased when you have a childlike faith that believes and clings to His promises as you journey through life. Experience anew Jesus's amazing, unconditional love as you trust and depend upon Him with the simple trust of a child.

Read Matthew 19:14
We are so blessed that You love each of us, Your children, without condition.

The Creator of the Universe

Lord, how Thy wonders are displayed wher'er I turn my eye,
if I survey the ground I tread or gaze upon the sky!

I Sing the Mighty Power of God by Isaac Watts

Earth is one of eight planets in our solar system, all circling the sun. The sun is one of the billions of stars in the Milky Way galaxy. And the Milky Way is one of the probable 200 billion galaxies in the universe. Each one of these galaxies likely has about the same amount of stars as the Milky Way.

Understanding the size of our world gives us new insight into the power of God. Our earth, including its high mountains, vast deserts, and deep oceans, seems big, but it is tiny when compared to the size of the universe. Yet our God—the One who loves us and died for us—created that universe and knows each of its stars by name. His power is unfathomable. His wonders are displayed wherever you look—the sea, the sky, the plains, the mountains...and the mirror.

Yes, in the mirror.

He loves and created you, making you one of His many wonders!

Read Psalm 139
Creator God, You are great, and Your power is beyond my comprehension.

His Outstretched Hand

His faithful follower I would be, for by His hand He leadeth me.
He Leadeth Me, O Blessed Thought by Joseph H. Gilmore

Surgery is risky. When patients sign waivers for their doctors to perform procedures, they are putting their lives in the hands of other people. Although they know surgery will be invasive and require days or even weeks of recovery, they trust the doctors' expertise and ability to restore their health.

God is more reliable than any doctor. We can think of Him as a specialist in spiritual health. His record is perfect, and even when His methods seem painful, they are ultimately in our best interests. The Great Physician nurtures us, monitors our progress, and ensures our ultimate well-being. Sometimes, as with physical conditioning, there is also emotional and spiritual recovery that will require us to be led by the hand of our supernatural Guide. He will give us newfound strength and lead us to restoration, fellowship, joy, and abundance.

Be His faithful follower. Grasp His hand.

Read Psalm 23:3
Lord, help me to let You lead.

Joyful News

Let those refuse to sing who never knew our God,
but children of the heav'nly King may speak their joys abroad.

COME, WE THAT LOVE THE LORD by Isaac Watts

It's hard to keep quiet about good news. It bubbles up inside us and we can't wait to share our joy with those closest to us. A new job, relationship, long-awaited pregnancy, or negative test results—each one is worth celebrating. Even life's little things, like a break in the weather or a good deal, are worth talking about.

How much more eager should we be, then, to tell others about the good news of Jesus Christ? After all, we have assurance of salvation from a mighty God who loved us so much He sacrificed His Son. He has made a way for us to be children of the King! We no longer have to struggle in our own strength to be good enough. Information this life changing is not meant to be kept to yourself—have you told anyone yet? Go speak your joy—everywhere!

Read Isaiah 35:6

Compel me to share the good news I have in You.

Come Visit

Gracious God, my heart renew.
GOD, BE MERCIFUL TO ME by Richard Redhead

A gracious hostess is always ready to meet the needs of her guests. Her hospitable words and actions express and demonstrate her focused desire to welcome those who enter her home.

God's graciousness toward us is much like that. All we have to do is show up at His "house." When we enter into His presence, He ministers to the needs of our soul. He welcomes us with a smile and invites us to sit and fellowship with Him. We share our hearts and He listens. Likewise, He shares His heart with us as we seek to know Him better and see where He is working in our world—and how we might join in.

When it's finally time to move along, we feel renewed and refreshed in spirit, and we're prepared to serve again. God is always a gracious host for our weary traveler hearts. Is it time for a long, leisurely visit with the host of heaven?

He's ready.

Read Psalm 51:10
O gracious Lord, please refresh my heart and renew my spirit.

Rock Solid

Great love of God, Jesus His name, He only is my foundation.
My Soul Finds Rest by Mary MacLean

Some of us grew up in church singing a song that contrasted the foolish man from Jesus's teachings who built his house upon the sand, and the wise man who built his house upon the rock. Accompanied by animated hand motions, we chirped, "The rains came down and the floods came up" three times. Then the final line of each respective verse announced the inevitable result: "The house on the sand went SMACK!" (shouted, of course, with hand claps for emphasis) while "the house on the rock stood firm."

The meaning of the song was as obvious to us then as it probably was to Jesus's listeners when they first heard the metaphor. If you build your life on anything other than Jesus Christ Himself, you will always suffer loss. But if you make Jesus your foundation, you can remain confident, regardless of what you face.

Is He your sure foundation?

Read Matthew 7:24–27
Lord, You're the only place to start. I'll build on You today.

Nail-pierced Hands

Thank You for the nail-pierced hands.
Worthy Is the Lamb by Darlene Zschech

American artist Lars Justinen created a sensitive interpretation of Christ's sacrifice in the oil painting *What Happened to Your Hand?* In this picture, a little girl innocently inquires about the nail mark in Jesus's outstretched hand. In so doing, she makes a discovery about God's greatest gift to mankind.

We adults aren't always so quick to ask the direct questions, but we do notice scars or disfigurement...and we wonder what happened. Sometimes the gruesomeness of another's wounds is almost too much for us; we turn away, not wanting to hear the story. But Jesus invites us to examine His scarred hands. He bids us ask what His wounds mean and why He let Himself suffer. Not so He can boast, and not so He can rub it in, but so that He can gently communicate a love beyond what we've ever known.

His outstretched arms are open wide for you, His nail-pierced hands reaching to lift you up to Him. Thank Him for His love for you today. Thank Him for His nail-pierced hands. Don't be afraid. Don't turn away. His are the wounds that heal.

Read John 20:25–29
For what You did to save me, Lord, I thank You.

The Holy Spirit

Fill Your church with joy overflowing.
HOLY SPIRIT COME by Kate Miner

When a new brother or sister joins our spiritual family, it's as if a new bowl is set beneath a constant, gentle waterfall. The Holy Spirit fills the believer to the point of overflowing, and keeps pouring into him.

The Holy Spirit was present at creation— we read that He hovered over the waters. When we accept Christ as our personal savior, we are born of the Spirit—and the very presence of God takes up residence in our believing hearts.

Jesus assured His followers that we would not be alone but that the Comforter would be with us forever. What a joy to have constant access to a God who guides and protects. May we always be thankful!

Read Colossians 3:10
Lord, thank You for the presence of the Holy Spirit, who reveals the Son to us and connects us with You.

Abba Father

Though He giveth or He taketh, God His children ne'er forsaketh.
CHILDREN OF THE HEAVENLY FATHER by Lina Sandell

What is the mark of a good father? Some would describe a good father as one who protects, provides for, and disciplines his children. The psalmist reminds us that a good father should also have compassion: "The Lord is like a father to his children, tender and compassionate to those who fear him" (Psalm 103:13 NLT).

A father's love is a powerful force. It was our heavenly Father's compassion that compelled Him to send His only Son to the cross to pay the price for our sins. Because of His love, He prepared a redemption plan—forgiving our worst offenses before we even asked—and made it possible for us to enjoy an ongoing, personal relationship with Him. Even when we disobey Him, reconciliation awaits through confession and repentance.

His desire to constantly be connected to us is a comfort. We have a loving and faithful God who will guide and protect us as we seek to follow Him.

Read Psalm 103
Your forgiving ways, dear Lord, allow me to have an unbroken relationship with You.

Report the News

I love to tell the story because I know 'tis true; it satisfies my longings as nothing else can do.

I LOVE TO TELL THE STORY by Katherine Hankey

Renowned broadcaster Paul Harvey Sr. was best known for his daily radio program *The Rest of the Story*. In each airing he grabbed your attention with an intriguing narrative, then delivered the payoff with an ending that made you think, *I never knew that.* You could tell by the inflection in his voice that even he got a kick out of the big finish.

When you listen to a friend recount a challenging scenario or share a situation in which they're awaiting a positive conclusion, do you just stand by and remain silent? Or are you chomping at the bit to tell them your story? As believers we have an incredible account of how Jesus brought us peace and redemption when we couldn't find hope for ourselves. We can offer our searching friends hope, the rest of The Story. There's no more powerful happy ending than that.

Read Acts 8:4

God, whether it's listening or telling that's needed, help me to be an encourager today.

Raise the Roof

O may we ever praise Him with heart and life and voice,
and in His blissful presence eternally rejoice!
Hosanna, Loud Hosanna by Jeanette Threlfall

Kids instinctively know how to rejoice. When they like something, they really let you know about it! Presented with a favorite treat or activity, they might spontaneously break out in a dance, twirl, squeal, or jump. Suddenly, you're the new favorite relative or family friend. Anyone who has been in a grocery store or park has witnessed such an event.

We adults could benefit from some of that enthusiasm. More often than not, we refrain from public merriment and boisterous celebration, fearing embarrassment. What would people think? Psychologists, however, credit an attitude of gratitude with improved physical health, mental clarity, and overall well-being.

When was the last time you employed your whole self—body, mind, will, emotions, and spirit—in childlike abandon to praising the Lover of your soul? Draw the curtains, crank up the music, and give it a try! Worship the King with the abandonment of a child.

Read Matthew 21:15–16
God, thank You for the opportunity to show
You how much I love You today.

Got Fear?

And in Your presence all our fears are washed away.

HOSANNA (PRAISE IS RISING) by Paul Baloche and Brenton Brown

So God has planted an idea on your heart. Are you nervous? Are you trying to figure out how to accomplish it? If you're still concerned after looking at your bank account, your contact list, and your resources, that's normal. Starting any new venture is risky.

However, this time you're not doing it on your own. This time, the dream is from Him—and the provision will be too. So instead of standing on your own two feet and trying to make it work out in your way, get down on your knees. Learn to get out of your head and into God's presence. Turn it over to Him and listen. The Lord will guide you; He will guard that dream; and He will remind you that He plans to do exactly what He promised. Now just ask Him to show you how you can help.

Read Psalm 16:11
Lord, protect this dream You've provided—and keep me from getting in Your way

Spiritual Uprising

May Your kingdom be established in our praises.
Blessed Be the Lord God Almighty by Bob Fitts

Earthly kingdoms are often established when a group of people becomes dissatisfied with their quality of life and seek to form something new. So it also goes in our spiritual lives. When we were lost, we wandered—seeking a sense of belonging and purpose. Thankfully, God provided a Savior...and with Him, a new realm in which to spend our lives. We are citizens of a spiritual world and servants of a leader that cannot be overthrown.

What difference does that make? As believers, His kingdom is alive in us. As we testify of His life-changing power and abiding love, as we serve others and demonstrate His love and compassion for people, the kingdom of Jesus will expand.

It's worth fighting for, and a secret worth sharing. Are you spreading the word? What sort of kingdom ambassador are you?

Read 2 Corinthians 1:3
Father, I am privileged to be an ambassador for Your kingdom. Enable me to represent You well.

Holy Intimacy

He sees all those tears that fall, and He'll hear you when you call.
He Knows My Name by Tommy Walker

God knows us thoroughly today. He knew us even before we were conceived. He devotes so much attention to the details of our existence that He has even numbered the individual hairs on our heads. (Some of us wish He'd count a few more!)

In the book of Isaiah we read that He will be with us our whole life long, even when we're old and gray. He cannot forget us because He keeps us engraved on the palms of His hands and writes our names in the Book of Life when we accept Christ as our personal Savior.

Scripture affirms that our God sits high and looks low; nothing escapes His notice. From His holy temple He hears our voice; our cries come into His ears. He knows our distress, hears every prayer, sees every tear, and knows every heart. He is the Word, and His promises are true.

Read Numbers 23:19
Lord, trusting You gives more comfort than anyone or anything else can provide.

God with Us

Emmanuel, God is with us, blessed Redeemer, living Word.
Jesus, Name above All Names by Naida Hearn

Jesus was God in our midst. He walked among the people, forming deep friendships with His followers, feeding the hungry, healing the sick, and redeeming the lost by taking the punishment for their sins. While these are past-tense terms, He is still "God with us" through the Holy Spirit.

Yet what if we didn't know the Living Word in a personal way? Just the thought of His absence in our lives makes us visualize a completely vacant and hopeless existence. Though many choose to live apart from God, when we consider what this world would be like if He were missing completely, we begin to picture a world filled with despair. Because God is love, every good and perfect gift comes from Him. If He were to remove Himself, then every good and loving experience would also be absent.

Fortunately, that is not the case. He is with us, blessed Redeemer, living Word.

Read Isaiah 9:6
Blessed Redeemer, thank You for Your presence from generation to generation.

Maximum Capacity

I'm pressed but not crushed, persecuted not abandoned, struck down but not destroyed.
Trading My Sorrows by Darrell Evans

You've seen the sign countless times: Maximum Capacity. Whether it's posted in an elevator, a vehicle, or even on a computer device, this warning declares the limits for safe operation.

Personally speaking, we sometimes feel as if we're operating at maximum capacity. When pressures start to mount, we cry out, "How much more I can take?"—asking it as much of God as anyone.

Fortunately, we can take God at His word, for He has promised that He will never give us more than we can handle. Though we sometimes feel alone and discouraged—as if the world around us is closing in—we can trust that God is helping us bear the load. That means we can bring our failures, our stresses, our heaviest burdens to Him. In fact, we can put all the weight on Him. He will never fail.

Read 2 Corinthians 4:8
You sustain me, God. What would I do without You?

The Spirit of Heaven

Friends will be there I have loved long ago; joy like a river around me will flow.
O That Will Be Glory for Me by Charles H. Gabriel

Heaven is a mysterious place. It plays a huge role in our faith lives, yet we have little specific information about it. We know we will have bodies in heaven, but what will we look like?

How will we recognize our fellow believers in Christ? Perhaps God didn't give us the details because they are beyond our comprehension. Heaven is so glorious, it is more than we could ever ask about or imagine.

While the mysteries of heaven won't be solved until we get there, the Holy Spirit provides a glimpse of God's glory here on earth. The Spirit that dwells in us is a daily reminder of what is to come and a personal promise that we are God's children. Through Him we occasionally hear whispers of miracles and catch tiny visions of what is to come.

We may not understand or be able to fully envision it, but we can trust the promises. Heaven will be a wonderful, joyful place!

Read Revelation 22:1–2

Thank You for Your promise of heaven. It gives me hope.

Bestseller

Tell me the story slowly, that I may take it in—
that wonderful redemption, God's remedy for sin.
TELL ME THE OLD, OLD STORY by Katherine Hankey

"Read it again...again...one more time. Please?"

Parents know the plea—they hear it every night from their children. "Won't you please read my favorite story?" There's something about those stories that makes kids feel secure. Perhaps part of the comfort is in hearing them expressed through someone they love.

If we're honest, we turn to Scripture for the same reasons. It's no coincidence that the Bible has sold more copies than any other book ever published. We never outgrow the reassuring stories and truths from a Father who loves us.

Thank God for the greatest story ever told—an epic adventure full of sacred romance, sacrificial love, heroic characters, and eternal virtues. It's a masterwork with a happy ending. And best of all, it's not fiction!

Have you shared that Story with your friends and family? Start telling it today; it just might become their new favorite.

Read 1 John 4:19
You have given us an epic story to tell, dear God. Help me relay it well.

Daily Devotion

Let every creature rise and bring His grateful honors to our King.

JESUS SHALL REIGN WHERE'ER THE SUN by Isaac Watts

History tells us that at the announcement of Christ's birth, the wise men set out to honor Him by personally greeting Him and bringing Him gifts. These wealthy, famous men likely traveled nearly a thousand miles and more than a year to reach the child. They carried special gifts of gold, frankincense, and myrrh to honor Jesus, the promised King, sent to save the world.

We don't have to go nearly that far to bring honor to our Lord. As we rise each day to face fresh challenges, we are presented with new opportunities to reflect His character through our behavior and speech. Regardless of our circumstances, we can intentionally offer our lives to His service in order that coworkers, friends, and family will see that He is a gracious and loving God. He considers that the greatest gift of all.

Read Psalm 72

My King, I praise You for reigning in my life.

Protection from My Enemies

So shall I be saved from my enemies.
I Will Call upon the Lord by Michael O'Shields

King David knew a thing or two about struggling with enemies. Over and over, David experienced God's protection of his life and his kingdom. He watched as his heavenly Father defeated and delivered him from his enemies. With God's help, David escaped with his life from King Saul's pursuit; he dodged a political coup launched by his own son, Absalom; he experienced military success against countless foreign threats. It is clear that David's enemies were unable to stand before God's chosen.

In this same way, today's Christians are God's chosen. Like King David, we can count on God's divine protection in our lives. No lies or deceptions strategized by our enemies can overpower the loving and benevolent protection provided by our God.

Read Psalm 18:3
Lord, remind me today that You have given me the strength to overcome any opposition.

Tell the World!

Shout it out, Jesus is alive, He's alive!
Happy Day—the Greatest Day in History by Tim Hughes and Ben Cantelon

January 31, 1865. July 21, 1969. November 9, 1989. Days that changed the world for the better. Whether the event was the abolition of slavery, man's first steps on the moon, or the destruction of the Berlin Wall, there's no disputing that these days altered our future course as citizens of planet Earth. To this day, we teach our children about these historical events and talk about their impact.

Now consider for a moment what Mary felt when she discovered that Jesus's body was missing from the tomb. Can you imagine the questions that flooded her mind? The hope that suddenly revived her grieving spirit? She ran to where the disciples were mourning, probably wanting to shout out the news.

Do you remember how you felt when you discovered that Jesus had conquered sin and death on your behalf? Did it radically change your life? Are you telling everyone you meet about the most incredible event in human history? After all, where would we be without it?

Read Matthew 16:16
Lord, thank You for making history.

Great God

Let all things their Creator bless, and worship Him in humbleness.
ALL CREATURES OF OUR GOD AND KING by Francis of Assisi

Were you to stand atop Mount Everest—the highest point on earth—you'd be at a loss to gauge the size of the entire planet, much less the larger universe we inhabit. Our eyes and minds simply cannot take it all in. We are not big enough.

Even from "lesser" vistas—as we stare at a patch of starry sky some evening or look out over a large city—we realize how small we are. But take heart. That little reality check also has an upside: it reveals how great God is. Humbling? Yes. But heartening too, because that great God also tenderly cares for you. He knows you by name. And He longs for your praise and worship.

Next time you're feeling small in the face of something that is far bigger than you, remember this: the majesty you can see doesn't begin to compare to the splendor of our God or the vastness of His love. Thank Him today. He is not only infinite, He is infinitely personal. And He cares for you.

Read Psalm 149:1
Dear Lord, I may be small, but great is Your love for me.

No More Darkness

Through You the darkness flees.
I Am Free by Jon Egan

Think of stepping into a dark room, flipping the light switch—and nothing happening. You know there's no way to get from the doorway to the reading lamp in the far corner without first bumping into the table, then a chair, before finally tripping over a stack of books. Yet once you get to that lamp and turn it on, darkness scatters. You turn and see exactly where everything is and you can safely make your way back across the room, this time without stumbling or bruising your shins.

When we walk with Jesus, we walk with a permanent light. The Bible says, "God is light," which means there can be no darkness in His presence. When you invited Jesus into your heart, His light caused all of the darkness there to flee. When you are faced with temptation, His light shines, showing the way out. When you feel the darkness of life is too much to bear, look up—He is the light that makes your darkness flee.

Read John 3:19–21

Thank You, Jesus, for shining Your light into my soul.

Will You Follow?

Where He leads me I will follow. I'll go with Him, with Him all the way.
WHERE HE LEADS ME by E. W. Blandy

When the Word of God was being written, travel was a difficult and dangerous endeavor. Instead of airplanes and cars, people had sandals and donkeys. Roads were long dirt paths through the wilderness. Bandits threatened travelers. Yet God required every Jewish adult male to make a pilgrimage to the temple in Jerusalem three times per year.

Depending on your perspective, obeying God's commands can be either a burden or a joy. You can serve out of grudging obligation or grateful obedience. Are you willing to follow where He leads? Ready to obey the commands clearly laid out in His Word? Prepared to follow the paths He shows you?

The Lord seeks willing hearts. You can trust Him to guide your steps through unknown territory; He promises to go before you.

Read Matthew 10:38–39
Dear God, help me to be a faithful follower.

Reality Check

Spirit, You're in me, You intercede and help in my need.
HEAVENLY FATHER, BEAUTIFUL SON by Mark Altrogge

Ever prayed for patience and found yourself stuck in a traffic jam? Ever prayed for financial accountability and then bounced a check? God was giving you a chance to practice what you prayed for. He was answering your prayer; it's just that sometimes He does it in ways you may not be expecting.

Our approach to prayer is to ask for what we think we need, but our focus is on the symptoms, not the root problem. Then we question why God doesn't seem to be listening.

Thank God for the Holy Spirit, who knows the heart of the Father, listens to the cries of our hearts, and knows how to reconcile the two so that we ultimately receive God's best.

Read Romans 8:26–27
Holy Spirit, thank You for seeing the good and perfect will of God completed in me.

Counting Down

Born to reign in us forever, now thy gracious kingdom bring.
COME THOU LONG-EXPECTED JESUS by Charles Wesley

As the end of the twentieth century approached, some folks predicted the end of the world. Probable system failures because of the rollover from 1999 to 2000 were referred to as the "Y2K bug." With great anticipation, the world braced for technology problems—system errors and widespread loss of information, potentially a massive system shutdown on multiple fronts—as the calendars turned to January 1, 2000. When the day arrived, few system failures occurred and new things captivated our interest.

Believers anxiously await the arrival of Jesus Christ, not with a sense of doom but of hope. With the promise of new life through Him, we often say, "Lord, come quickly." When Jesus comes He will bring eternal peace, joy, and the fulfillment of God's amazing plan.

Have you shared the news? As His children, we have reason to eagerly anticipate Jesus's promised return, but let's not keep the details to ourselves.

Read Acts 13:32–34
I am so grateful for Your promise to return for us, Jesus.

Two Words

I know He rescued my soul, His blood has covered my sins. I believe.
My Redeemer Lives by Reuben Morgan

What two words did Jesus say to Jairus when his daughter lay dying? He could have said, "I'm sorry," or "I can't," or "I'm busy." But instead He said, "Just believe." In spite of Jairus's circumstances, his twelve-year-old's worsening condition, and even additional interruption, Jesus told Jairus to just believe. Notice the word *just.* It means "simply" or "purely." In other words, "the least one can do." At the report of his daughter's death, the man was told to "just" believe. According to Jesus, that was enough. Despite the fact that faith was fighting against all odds, it was enough.

Next time you find yourself in a seemingly impossible situation, challenge yourself to "just believe." After all, you have an overabundance of evidence that God is powerful; you've already seen what He can do in a person's life. Just believe. And keep believing. He is always faithful.

Read Luke 8:50
Lord, help me to just believe.

Life Giver

Words of life and beauty, teach me faith and duty.
WONDERFUL WORDS OF LIFE by Philip P. Bliss

God's promise to never leave or forsake us provides assurance of abundant life and grants the strength to continually strive to do His will by faith. Our mission and privilege is to love Him with all our heart, mind, and will. In doing so, we glorify Him and inspire others to come before the throne of grace.

His Word, the Bible, is a testament to His great power and love for mankind. In chapter after chapter—from Genesis to Revelation—our Lord gives us instruction for living and promises protection and provision to whoever will follow Him. In the Old Testament, He provided His people with the manna they needed for each day. What an incredible demonstration of His care for the most basic needs! Yet the Israelites struggled to follow His seemingly simple instruction to trust.

In what ways do you need to follow Him by faith today? Don't lose heart. He will give you the manna you need.

Read John 6:63
Thank You for the promises in Your Word, Lord. Help me to faithfully follow You.

Eclipse of Doubt

Melt the clouds of sin and sadness, drive the dark of doubt away.
JOYFUL, JOYFUL, WE ADORE THEE by Henry van Dyke

When a total solar eclipse occurs, the light of the sun gets completely blocked by the moon. For these few minutes, day is turned to night. But when the eclipse ends, the sun resumes its shining.

Sometimes the sorrows of life can cause spiritual eclipses in our lives, turning everything upside down. When tragedy and grief occur, most of us automatically question why God allows such horrible things to happen. We allow circumstances to create clouds of doubt that shroud us in darkness. In spite of these doubts, though, the light of God and His truth still shines brightly. No eclipse can completely hide Him!

In your times of sorrow, invite Him to remove your doubts so that you may see clearly again. Then consider asking God to help you to see your circumstances through His eyes instead of defining Him through your circumstances.

Read 2 Samuel 22:29
Help me to remember that Your light exists despite my doubts, God.

Divine Rest

Breathe, o breathe Thy loving Spirit into every troubled breast;
let us all in Thee inherit, let us find Thy promised rest.
LOVE DIVINE, ALL LOVES EXCELLING by Charles Wesley

Professing Christ is no guarantee of a problem-free life. In fact, some would say that the closer your relationship with Christ, the more problems you may encounter. It's easy to rest in God's grace in good times, but how do you react during tough times?

Our pride reveals itself in our tendency to take matters into our own hands rather than trust God. The Bible assures us we will have trials and tribulations (1 Peter 1:5–7). Yet the key is to endure these challenges in such a way that God is glorified.

Are you facing problems today? Surrender your burdens, concerns, and fears into Christ's loving and capable hands. Rather than trying to manipulate circumstances that are beyond your control, commit your life to God's care, purposes, and timing. When you put yourself in His trustworthy hands, you will find rest.

Read 1 John 4:9
Heavenly Father, teach me to lean on You and place all my trust in you.

Surprise!

I know not when my Lord may come, at night or noon-day fair,
nor if I walk the vale with Him or meet Him in the air.
I Know Whom I Have Believed by Daniel W. Whittle

Surprises—some of us adore them, always eager for the next. And some of us go to great lengths to avoid anything that isn't on our carefully maintained calendar. Yet there's one "surprise" we'll all embrace: the coming of the Lord. That glorious day will usher in the end of this age with trumpet blasts, angelic hosts, and the arrival of the King of kings. Every knee will bow. Every tongue will confess: Jesus is Lord.

Christ's return is one surprise party we'll be happy to attend. And even better...it's a party with an open guest list; there's room at the banquet table for more. So let's get busy telling people about the celebration to come, encouraging everyone we meet to get ready.

Thankfully, we need not worry about the details of the day, time, or location. We need only to be ready to welcome the Surprise of the Ages when the trumpet sounds.

Read 2 Timothy 1:12
Lord, help me spread the word about Your forthcoming party of parties.

almighty allies

Lord of Glory, You have called me friend.
Friend of God by Michael Gungor and Israel Houghton

The name of a prominent man in the Bible is linked with God and the word friend: Abraham.

Abraham became God's friend by allowing his faith and his actions to work together. God credited this to him as righteousness. He was a man as mortal and flawed as we are, but Abraham displayed absolute, unwavering faith through his obedience to God. His heart and actions were in accord. Had God not intervened, Abraham would have surrendered his beloved Isaac on the altar as God asked of him. He was ready to do anything that God requested, showing us what it means to be a true friend of the Father.

Christ, Lord of all, is our sacrificial Lamb. He shed His blood and forfeited His life so that we can boldly come into God's presence, speak with Him, and be called both child and friend of God.

Read Hebrews 4:15–16

Holy Spirit, teach me to listen for and obey Your voice without question.

Highly Favored

O that with yonder sacred throng we at His feet may fall!
We'll join the everlasting song and crown Him Lord of all.
ALL HAIL THE POWER OF JESUS' NAME by Edward Perronet

What makes a group of people blessed? Is it living in the right neighborhood—a peaceful "gated" community that houses luxurious mansions? Rubbing elbows with those who are in the spotlight?

Or could it be that it's their humble service and the object of their worship that makes them special? Our hearts fill with hope at that thought. Perhaps we can approach the throne just as we are—accepted, because Jesus humbled Himself. Just the thought of joining in the roar of a cheering heaven is almost unimaginable.

Whether we just took a meal to an elderly neighbor or sang with all our hearts in worship today, every one of us is welcome—expected, even—to bow at His feet in adoration because Jesus, our Redeemer, made it possible. Praise Him—for the deliverer of our souls has made our everyday offerings sacred.

Read Philippians 2:9–11
Lord, thank You for accepting my worship.

Rescued from Ourselves

With His blood He has saved me; with His pow'r He has raised me;
to God be the glory for the things He has done.
My Tribute by Andrae Crouch

What a blessing to know that we don't have to figure out how to save ourselves—that it took sacrifice greater than any penance and grace more profound than we could produce. There was no way for us to work hard enough or be good enough to achieve what only our Savior could accomplish.

In Isaiah, we learn that our inconsistent attempts at righteousness are like filthy rags. We see this in our personal lives. We intend to do the right thing yet we forget to pray for our spouse as we promised, lose our patience with strangers in traffic, and try to push through our own agenda without consideration of others.

Mercifully, God graciously provided His perfect Son, Jesus, as our Redeemer. Because of this, our salvation is assured. This doesn't mean we don't attempt to do well, to honor His name. We must still strive for excellence. But regardless of our accomplishments, we can rest in God's grace.

Read Psalm 115:1
Help me to be mindful of the nearness of Your great mercy at every moment.

The Only Constant

Age to age You're still the same by the power of the name.
El Shaddai by Michael Card and John Thompson

There is an old saying, "The only thing that's constant is change." As true as that might be about life, it's not true of our God. Thankfully, the foundation of trust on which we build a personal relationship with the Lord is anchored in His unchanging character. The Bible testifies that age-to-age God is still the same. Hebrews 13:8 tells us that Jesus Christ is the same yesterday, today, and forever. He is ever faithful to complete what He has committed to do. Praise God for these truths!

God is truth. His motives are pure. His justice is fair. His mercy is boundless. His love is unending, and no boundary of space, time, or distance restricts Him from fulfilling His holy Word. He always was, always is, and always will be El Shaddai, God Almighty.

Read Genesis 17:1
My soul is anchored in Your faithfulness, Lord.
I am secure in Your unchanging love.

Ready, Willing, and Able

Melt me, mold me, fill me, use me.
Spirit of the Living God by Daniel Iverson

Whether it's an artistic vase or a functional pitcher for water, no potter's work is ever complete until it has been fired in a kiln. Without the refining fire, it will crack and fall apart and fail to accomplish its purpose. Without that important finishing process, the craftsman's work would never be fit for the art gallery, much less a dinner table.

Becoming a vessel for God's glory is a process in which He continually melts away our impurities, the way intense heat brings dross to the surface when precious metals are refined. The Potter's hands shape us for service through the gifts given to us by the Holy Spirit.

It's an incredible privilege to share the hope of Christ and sow His love throughout this hurting world. Choosing to be "used" starts with a willing, humble spirit. Pray today and ask God to prepare you for service; then get ready to see Him accomplish His will through you.

Read Acts 11:5
I'm Yours, Lord; use me.

How We Thank God

Let us then be true and faithful, trusting, serving every day.
WHEN WE ALL GET TO HEAVEN by Eliza E. Hewitt

No one can match God's loving-kindness or repay Him for His grace and mercy, but we can thank Him with our faithfulness, exhibiting trust and service every day. No matter what happens on our job, in class, or at home, God is in control. Political unrest, financial chaos, military conflicts—nothing catches God by surprise. Because He knows, we don't have to worry.

We can prayerfully begin our day, committing to submit our will to His and intentionally seeking opportunities to share His love. Being a blessing to others requires putting "self" at the bottom of the list and opening our hearts to the cares and concerns of others. It means talking less and listening more.

It means looking beyond the callous things others may say or do and recognizing the hurt in them. Their pain is actually our opportunity to show them the Jesus inside of us—and the healing He offers.

Read 1 Thessalonians 4:7
Lord Jesus, prepare me to serve You today.

Prayer: The Map to God

Help me find the way; bring me back to You.

DRAW ME CLOSE by Kelly Carpenter

Anyone who has ever been lost knows the value of a map. These days we rely on GPS to guide us to our destinations.

In the life of the believer, we discover that it's only in seeking God that we find Him. And in learning to hear His voice and discern His direction, we discover the holiest map of all.

While we frequently close our prayers with petitions and requests, most of us begin our prayers by acknowledging God as "Father," "Lord," or "Savior." When we establish that He is the Creator and we are merely the creation, we find our "You are here" spot on the map. As we continue in prayer, we thank and praise God for His goodness and hone in on His voice as our compass, nodding in a certain direction.

We often think of praying as a means to an end, of getting something we want or need, yet in its finest hour, prayer is a way for the believer to draw closer to God and find His path for us.

Read 1 John 2:6

Continue to draw me closer to You each day, wherever You're leading me.

Revering the King

He's high and lifted up. Heaven and earth adore.
God So Loved by Reuben Morgan

In Disney's *The Lion King*, Mufasa the ruler held up his cub Simba, the future ruler, high above his shoulders—on display for his entire kingdom to worship. By doing so, every citizen understood his position as royalty and revered him as such.

In today's society, it is difficult to find a sense of holiness in the world, and occasionally it's even challenging to spot it in the church. Sometimes we enter church with the same casual air we might have entering a nightclub. We talk and pass notes during praise and worship. We doze off or exchange text messages during the sermon. It appears we have lost reverence for Him and the place where we go to worship Him in community with other believers. Have we forgotten that the God we serve is holy?

May all His creation honor Him with the esteem He is due.

Read John 3:16
You and you alone are my sovereign King.
Please rule and reign in my life.

Christlike Thinking

God in my thinking, God in my speaking. Be my everything.
Everything by Tim Hughes

Right thinking. It may sound simple, but that doesn't mean it's easy. When we accept Jesus Christ as our Lord and Savior, our thought life does not change immediately. For example, we don't automatically stop thinking unkind thoughts about others.

The goal is to think as our Savior does, with as much love, respect, and grace as He has in His heart for others, and with an ear attuned to God's direction. But we're still learning to listen for God's voice so He can direct our thoughts. Paul declared, "Let this mind be in you which was also in Christ Jesus" (Philippians 2:5 NKJV). So we know

it's possible. But having Christ's mind means total surrender of our selfish desires and submission to His Word, His will, His way.

It's been said that imitation is the sincerest form of flattery. Who better for us to imitate than Jesus? As believers, we have all the tools we need to renew our minds and honor Him through our deeds. And adopting Christ's thinking will allow God's presence and power in our lives to become fully present.

Read Philippians 2:5
Guide me in all of my thoughts and actions, Lord.

Peace, Be Still

Even though I walk through the valley of the shadow of death,
Your perfect love is casting out fear.
You Never Let Go by Matt and Beth Redman

At the height of the Civil Rights struggle, on the steps of Birmingham's Sixteenth Street Baptist Church where four black girls were killed in a bombing, Dr. Martin Luther King Jr. said, "The reason I can't follow the old eye-for-an-eye philosophy is that it ends up leaving everybody blind."

As believers, we are most like God when we exercise unmerited love. It's easy to love our friends, but the true test of Christian maturity is the ability to love our enemies. Dr. King's statement brings to mind how Jesus responded when He stepped out of the boat and calmed the sea. In the midst of the storm, He called for peace.

When you feel most powerless, take comfort in the fact that God is in control, and live to exhibit His love through your every action.

Read Matthew 5:39
Lord, in my darkest hour I pray I will still reflect Your light.

Final Resting Place

Sickness and sorrow, pain and death are felt and feared no more.
I am bound for the Promised Land.

On Jordan's Stormy Banks by Samuel Stennett

Saying good-bye to dying loved ones is never easy because it seems so final. But is it really?

Scripture reveals that for the believer, death is not the end of life but rather a beginning. Heaven is our incomparable Promised Land. Our home. Our place of relief from earth's sickness, sorrow, pain, and death. Within its gates, earth's weary sojourners find sweet rest in the presence of their heavenly Father. There, Love vanquishes the rejection we've experienced in this life. There, Peace overcomes strife. There, Hope conquers despair.

"I am going home" takes on a new meaning when whispered at death's door by one who has confessed Jesus as Savior.

God's Word is true: Heaven is real. Eternity and all its graces are just a breath away. Believe that this farewell is more of a "see you soon" than a "good-bye."

Read Hebrews 4:11

Lord, help me to rejoice as You welcome my brothers and sisters into the Promised Land.

Pining Away

I want You more than gold or silver, only You can satisfy.
As the Deer by Marty Nystrom

Luke 10:27 may be the Bible's most challenging verse. With just a few poignant words Jesus instructs us to embrace God with no less than our whole heart and love others as much as we love ourselves.

Do you want God more than gold and Jesus's sweet fellowship more than silver?

Some intentionally—and others inadvertently—compartmentalize their lives in such a way that the person at Wednesday's Bible study or Sunday service bears little resemblance to who they are at work, in the community, or in the privacy of their homes. They struggle between their heart's desire and the flesh that seeks, in vain, for earthly contentment. But longings of the soul can only be satisfied by giving complete obedience to the Holy Spirit.

Do you wish to love Him with all your heart, mind, and strength? Pray and ask God today to align your cravings with His will. He will answer by renewing your mind and changing your heart.

Read Psalm 42:1–2
Lord, help me to hunger only for You.

Redeemed

How wide, how deep, how great is Your love for me.
AMAZED by Jared Anderson

We do not have to try to win God's affection because we are born surrounded by God's love. We need only open our arms to accept Christ as our Savior. Nothing we have ever done or thought is hidden from God's sight. So vast and irrevocable is His love that—in spite of what we consider to be our darkest and most secret sins—He still calls us to come to Him.

Jesus, our Redeemer, paid the price to free us by shedding His precious blood. If we will hand over our sins to Him, we will be cleansed and restored. The horrors of past sin can no longer bind us once we repent and allow Him to shelter us in His life-giving embrace.

For us, He conquered sin and defeated death; truly nothing can ever separate us from Him again.

Read Ephesians 3:14–19
Jesus, You see me in my sins but still you want to love and bless me. Your love is amazing!

Heavenly Delight

But when the world has seen the light, they will dance with joy.
I Could Sing of Your Love Forever by Martin Smith

Children know how to be enthusiastic. As soon as they find out plans have been made for a special outing, they ask about it every day—at least once. That's why parents often decide to surprise their kids with a trip to Disney. The unbridled excitement that overcomes them at the "great reveal" is priceless; and of course, at the same time they've spared themselves weeks of the question "When are we going?"

How eager are you to behold Jesus in heaven? You know it's coming. Are you talking about it every day with the people around you? Reminding everyone that it's getting closer by the day? The Bible says that when we see Him we will glorify and worship Him. We will sing, dance, and praise Him. We will shout with exuberant joy. Oh, what a day it will be....

Read Revelation 22:5
God, help me to share my enthusiasm for our heavenly reunion to come.

Giving to Get

Pardon for sin and a peace that endureth, Thine own dear presence to cheer and to guide.
GREAT IS THY FAITHFULNESS by Thomas O. Chisholm

Peace can be elusive as we try to live in this world but not of it. "When unable to rest, one should not count sheep but talk to the Shepherd" is an insightful adage! Only when we humble ourselves—carrying our failures and concerns to Christ—can the issues that plague our hearts be relinquished to God's keeping for enduring peace.

What a blessing! We are pardoned when we offer Him our bruised and battered hearts filled with fear, sin, and guilt. Our God then washes us clean and enables us to thrive in peace because we have become new creations in Him. That's because the Holy Spirit resides in us, giving us access to our Father's presence to comfort and His wisdom to guide.

What a faithful God! He not only covers sin with His love but leaves part of Himself within us so that we never need to feel lost, afraid, or alone again.

Read Lamentations 3:22–23
I trust everything in every day to You, God.

True Riches

Let the poor say, "I am rich because of what the Lord has done for us."
GIVE THANKS by Henry Smith, Jr.

Jesus left behind the riches of heaven in order to clothe Himself in mortal flesh. He willingly experienced degradation, betrayal, persecution, and immeasurable pain in order to redeem our sin-sick souls. Through Him, for those willing to accept it, the wages of sin and death have been replaced with the greatest riches of all, eternal life in God's kingdom.

In Scripture, stories like that of the repentant thief on the cross, the widow's mite, and the beggar Lazarus illustrate that Christ's sacrifice enables even those who are materially poor in this life to have crowns and mansions waiting in heaven. In Christ, even the physically weak can have hearts filled with mustard-seed faith that makes them strong enough to move mountains.

Our God does not use earthly scales to assign values. It is the state of our hearts that most concerns Him. What is the state of yours?

Read 2 Corinthians 8:9
Lord, I love You—not just for what You've done already but for what You will do.

Covered by Grace

Grace flows down and covers me.
Grace Flows Down by David Bell, Louie Giglio, and Rod Pageant

For any cook, pulling together Thanksgiving dinner is stressful. You want everything to be timed right and turn out perfectly. From the turkey and dressing to the salads and dessert, it's a formidable challenge to prepare a flawless meal that will impress in-laws or friends. At times like this, be thankful for gravy. Humorous as it may be, many a cook has relied on gravy to cover the embarrassment of a dry bird or bland potatoes.

While countless theologians have sought to define grace, and even more books have been written to describe it, simply said, God's grace is a lot like that holiday gravy: He covers us with it. Only with grace, it's not an optional add-on; it's essential. We come to our Savior in need, lacking the ability to satisfy the cravings of our own soul or live as perfected believers. But our heavenly Father pours grace over us through Jesus—and suddenly we are worthy to be used to accomplish His plan.

Read Ephesians 4:7–13
Great God, thank You for covering me with Your grace today.

Spacious Living

For the love of God is broader than the measure of man's mind.
THERE'S A WIDENESS IN GOD'S MERCY by Frederick W. Faber

Eternity is impossible for humans to fully grasp. Everything in our mortal experience has both a beginning and an end. Similarly, we find it challenging to understand God's depth of love for us. To meditate on God and all He's done to provide us with abundant life is to know the true meaning of thanksgiving.

He showed us the distance He was willing to go, of course, through the sacrifice of His Son. Are you unnecessarily continuing to carry burdens of guilt because your mind cannot conceive of the depth and breadth of God's mercy? Mercy that removed all your transgressions as far as the east is from the west? Once you repent, also forgive yourself. God already has. And He doesn't make mistakes.

Read Romans 8:38–39
Merciful Savior, thank You for a love so great, it is beyond human understanding.

Glory on High

For Thou, O Lord, art high over all the earth.
I Exalt Thee by Pete Sanchez, Jr.

High above the earth God sits enthroned. He is so magnificent, so beyond us—and yet, miraculously, with us—that His splendor calls to all things, seen and unseen. Planets, stars, and entire galaxies were spoken into creation with but a whisper from God. The heavens themselves reflect and bear witness to God's glory.

But God is even greater than His creation. He outshines the sun, moon, stars, and every other heavenly body. His glory fills the whole world, all at once, every day. He fills us. The Holy Spirit beckons us to explore God's brilliance through worship, prayer, and study of the Word. He ushers us into God's glorious presence, where we have no fear of condemnation or rebuke.

What an amazing Creator we serve. Glory to God on high!

Read Psalm 95:3
Lord, help me be aware of Your glory, high above and here below.

Lavish Love

Spread His praise from shore to shore, how He came to pay
our ransom through the saving cross He bore.
O the Deep, Deep Love by Bob Kauflin

The amazing thing about God's love is that it is lavished on us in spite of an intimate knowledge of who we are. It's easy to love someone before we know about their quirks, shortcomings, and vices. It's easy to love someone before that person fails or hurts us. Yet even before God created the world, He knew that we would sin, that we would turn our backs on Him. Before God walked with Adam in the Garden of Eden, He knew He would one day sweat blood for us in the Garden of Gethsemane. Before God breathed life into Adam's nostrils, He knew He would one day give His own life to buy us back.

A love that pays our ransom on the cross of salvation—with complete knowledge of who we truly are—is indeed a love deeper than we will ever be able to fathom!

Read Romans 5:6–8
Jesus, help me rest today in the knowledge that You love me completely.

Life's Song

I can sing in troubled times; sing when I win.
HOW CAN I KEEP FROM SINGING by Chris Tomlin, Ed Cash, and Matt Redman

Scientists say that birds sing to make their presence known. They don't sing simply for the joy of it but to signal other birds to stay away from their partner or territory—or to attract one of their own. Each species has a particular song that distinguishes it from others.

Why do you sing (even if it's only in your heart—or in the shower)? Martin Luther once wrote, "When I cannot pray, I sing." As believers, we often use hymns and praise songs to call out to God. When we find ourselves at a loss for words, the songwriter's lyrics become our script.

Whether in grief or joy, sometimes it's difficult to find the words to express our passion. So go ahead—use the songwriter's prose to help you call out to the Father. He is listening for you.

Read Ephesians 5:19
Lord, thank You for the gift of music that allows me to express my feelings.

Faking It?

We've a Savior to show to the nations who the path of sorrow hath trod,
that all of the world's great peoples might come to the truth of God.
We've a Story to Tell to the Nations by H. Ernest Nichol

"Fake it till you make it" is the guiding principle of wannabes. They have few, if any, qualms about acting like something they are not.

Jesus, on the other hand, was no fraud. From start to finish, He told the truth about His humanity and divinity. He chose to live candidly, allowing the world to bear witness to His life—if people had eyes to see. He shared everything from great sorrow to joy, living authentically among us.

Sharing our testimonies is one way we can be equally real. Rather than sugarcoat the trials and traumas we've endured, we can opt to vulnerably share our real-life stories of God's grace through it all—good and bad. Doing so leads people to the truth of God, and to saving faith.

What's your story? Tell it. Someone might need to know you truly understand a measure of their sorrow and pain, in order to accept the elixir you offer: Jesus Christ.

Read Matthew 28:19
Lord, help me to be Your authentic servant to everyone I meet.

Safe and Secure in Jesus

No pow'r of hell, no scheme of man, can ever pluck me from His hand.
In Christ Alone by Stuart Townend

Deadbolt locks on doors, burglar bars on windows, password-protected files—each one is an example of the safety and security we try to establish for ourselves. As believers, however, we discover our only true security is found in our Lord and Savior Jesus Christ.

He makes us secure, not just for eternity but in the day-to-day moments of our lives. Sometimes tragedy will befall us; sometimes accidents will happen. People will betray us, and we will make mistakes too. It all comes with the territory of living in a fallen world.

Yet the security we are promised in Christ covers us in all things. We can rest assured that no matter what happens, nothing has reached us randomly. Our circumstances have been sifted through the hands of the One who loves us most—the One who has committed to keep us in His care now and for eternity.

Read John 10:28

I am blessed by the security You've given me through Your Son, Jesus.

RSVP

Time is now fleeting, the moments are passing, passing from you and from me.
Softly and Tenderly by Will L. Thompson

Technology offers many time savers, enabling us to squeeze as much from—and into—a day as possible; however, we still cannot control time. Days, weeks, and months continue to pass, seemingly faster and faster every year.

Lovingly, Jesus urgently pleads to all of us to come to Him. He supplies us with the presence of mind and opportunity to make the one decision that impacts eternity. None of us, young or old, is promised tomorrow. There's no guarantee of an "average" life span of seventy years. The improbable, unanticipated, or accidental may be just around the corner or within the next heartbeat. There is only one certainty: Jesus.

Why delay and ignore God's mercies? Procrastination, convincing us that there is plenty of time to respond, is perhaps Satan's most effective deceit. Promptly answer Jesus's invitation. He is watching and waiting to pardon all sins and give life everlasting.

Read Matthew 11:28
Lord, nothing this world offers can compare to life with You in heaven.

Storm Protection

Thou wast their rock, their fortress, and their might.
Thou, Lord, their captain in the well-fought fight.
FOR ALL THE SAINTS by William W. How

As the person in charge of a vessel, a captain has command over all who are on board his ship, and his firm command provides a sense of security for the passengers. If a storm arises, the crew draws confidence from their captain's experience and authority. The storm may be fierce, but they know their captain will see them safely to port.

Similarly, God is the captain over our lives, and nothing can rise against Him that He can't conquer. God is our stronghold—our rock, fortress, and deliverer. No matter how fierce the storm appears, we can trust in Him.

Praise God that He has all authority over heaven and earth. Because we are the children of God, we can call on Him, and He will fight our battles.

Read Hebrews 11:16
I will trust you to be my fortress.

Hearing God's Heartbeat

O Jesus, blest Redeemer, sent from the heart of God,
hold us who wait before Thee, near to the heart of God.
NEAR TO THE HEART OF GOD by Cleland B. McAfee

Kittens are comforted by the rhythm of a heartbeat. When they're born, their eyes are like buttonholes. They can't see yet and they are easily frightened. Even when they're held by loving hands, their small, fuzzy bodies squirm in fear, attempting to escape. Yet if they allow the person holding them to draw them close, they can find comfort in the sound of a beating heart. The heartbeat reminds them of being safe in their mother's womb.

God does not want to keep us at arm's length. He desperately desires to hold us close to His heart. When we stop struggling against His will and love, we can find comfort in His arms. Like kittens, we may not be able to see exactly where we are, but we will be able to feel the blessed reassurance of His tender care and compassion.

Jesus, your Redeemer, holds you close to His heart. Draw near and be at peace.

Read James 4:8
Hold me close to Your heart, precious Redeemer.

Praise Him

Does sadness fill my mind? A solace here I find, may Jesus Christ be praised!
MAY JESUS CHRIST BE PRAISED by Edward Caswall

What a consolation to know that regardless of the turbulence that life may bring, we have a steadfast, loving Savior. Even when sadness overwhelms us like a powerful wave, God is worthy of all praise.

Seems like a contradiction, doesn't it? And yet, when we hear survivors of life's worst circumstances profess that God was with them, when they can bear witness that God is good, there is something in their words that rings true.

We never know how God will provide for us in our time of need. But He does. And He will. Sometimes He will comfort us through others. Sometimes He will send unexpected deliverance. Always, He will patiently abide with us through the valley. Though we may feel alone, we are not alone. He is with us to the end—our solace and strength. What a tender Savior we serve.

Like Job, when we choose to trust His goodness anyway, when we choose to find a way to praise Him in the worst of circumstances, He will be glorified. We will be blessed. And He will inhabit our praise.

Read Romans 9:5
I long to believe in Your goodness, Lord, even when circumstances are not good.

Title?

You're my supply, my breath of life.
Enough by Chris Tomlin and Louie Giglio

It's easy to forget that it's only by God's grace that we can accomplish anything—even simple tasks. Even our abilities and strengths come from God.

Zerubbabel learned that we can't stack up righteous deeds without a divine hand holding ours. When he labored to rebuild the temple, God reminded him: "Not by might, nor by power, but by my Spirit, says the Lord of hosts" (Zechariah 4:6 ESV).

Pride puffs up, but worship gives up, surrendering glory in every good deed as an act of worship. It's only by God's grace that we stand at all. Therefore, we owe every breath and every step to God. Our only posture should be thanksgiving and praise.

We don't make progress unless He enables us. As you check items off your to-do list, worship God in loving communion, saying, "This, too, is for You."

Read Psalm 33:20

Jesus, teach us to practice Your presence, doing everything unto You.

Wedding Plans

And oh, we will stand by his side, a strong, pure, spotless bride.
WE WILL DANCE by David Ruis

A woman's wedding day is one of the most anticipated days of her life. In many cases, she's dreamed of every detail—from the dress and ring to the flowers and cake. From an early age, girls imagine walking down the aisle, before family and friends, toward a strong, handsome groom who is awaiting her arrival.

Each of us who has accepted Christ by faith is preparing to one day meet Him. And because of His great love for us, our Savior awaits the arrival of His bride, the Church, whom He has redeemed and restored.

How are you preparing for this grand reunion? Like that young girl who is focused on the day she will meet her groom, are you carefully planning your steps to the day you will meet your Groom? He promises to come back for His bride. Are you ready?

Read Ephesians 5:25–27
Lord, I want to be ready when You come. Prepare my heart.

Brothers and Sisters

Join hands then, brothers of the faith, whate'er your race may be;
who serves my Father as a son is surely kin to me.
In Christ There Is No East or West by John Oxenham

If you've never considered how different life in other societies is from our own, the chance to participate in a short-term mission becomes more than an incredible service opportunity; it's also a remarkable learning experience.

India, Haiti, Russia, Turkey—each nation is vastly different from the United States. Yet remarkably, we share one basic human condition: our need for a Savior. How sweet can be the fellowship and unity among believers when we share not only new cultural experiences but also our gratitude to a heavenly Father who is powerful enough to connect us, regardless of language or culture.

Happily, we can enjoy similar experiences without boarding an airplane. Consider linking up with a church in a neighboring community to worship or serve those in need. Watch and see how the Lord can use the differences among His people for a mighty, unified purpose.

Read Acts 10:35
Help me to join together with Your people,
Lord, to serve and worship.

Keep Love Alive

I'll love Thee in life; I will love Thee in death,
and praise Thee as long as Thou lendest me breath.

My Jesus, I Love Thee by William R. Featherston

Have you ever fallen in love? How did it happen? Most couples can remember exactly when and where love happened for them. How about your love story with God? Has it been written yet?

The greatest of all love stories is His romance with us. He courted us. Made the first move. Fell in love with us before we even noticed Him. God's love met us at the cradle, and will reach for us at the grave. It is always there, whether we realize it or not.

It's easy to take something so sure and steady for granted. That's one of the dangers couples must sidestep the longer they are married. As believers, we face a similar temptation. For the sake of your relationship with God, resist it. Nurture your love for Him. Keep it vibrant and strong. Protect it from the opinions of those who neither know nor love Him. After all, it is your story, and yours to tell.

Today, don't hesitate to share how you fell in love with God, and how He fell in love with you first.

Read 1 John 4:19
God, help me to fall deeper in love with You, day by day.

Peace

Perfect submission, all is at rest, I in my Savior am happy and blest.
BLESSED ASSURANCE by Fanny J. Crosby

When US Air flight 1509 crashed into the Hudson River on that cold January day, not one of the 154 passengers was harmed. Incredibly, there were no major injuries. The passengers knew they were fortunate, but one said, "It is a miracle that we needed." This man realized he was blessed to be alive! The courage and capability of the flight crew wowed everyone, but at least one acknowledged that God had been present with them too.

Because we as believers submit to God, we have access to peace and confidence in the face of tragedy, trauma, and turmoil. We can trust in His promises—the blessings for all believers—and simply rest in His care. Though it takes faith, when we surrender our will and place our dependence on God, rather than the things of man, He provides peace.

Read Acts 17:31
God, You provide rest for my battered heart. It's just one of the reasons I need You!

Power in Weakness

*Make friends of God's children; help those who are weak,
forgetting in nothing His blessing to seek.*
TAKE TIME TO BE HOLY by William D. Longstaff

While the world rarely celebrates vulnerability, Jesus applauds our transparency. Authentic love helps to sustain us all during seasons of frailty. Some days we need help navigating stormy seas with waves that threaten to take us under. On other days we are aboard the ship, tossing out a life ring to others. In either case, a silver lining of blessing pushes through adversity's cloud.

Our Savior modeled strength in weakness. He proved spiritual strength triumphs over physical, emotional, or mental weakness. He showed compassion and caring to friends and enemies alike, and taught us to rely upon one another. Jesus didn't keep a "stiff upper lip"—He wept, and He sees our tears now. In our weakness and desperation, we allow Him to come closer.

Helping others experiencing weakness extends Jesus's earthly ministry. Be available. Rely on God's strength. Seek his blessing. Respond with faith, not criticism. Show compassion, aiding everyone you meet with tender, humble, loving care. Just as Jesus loves us.

Read Hebrews 12:14
Father, I want to help. Please show me how.

Promises Fulfilled

You rule, You reign, You said You're coming back again.
ALL THE EARTH WILL SING YOUR PRAISES by Paul Baloche

"I promise" carries a magnitude of responsibility. But rather than being a solemn verbal agreement to follow through with corresponding action, it's almost become a cliché today. People make promises then break them when it's no longer convenient. Our ability to share our faith hinges on our integrity.

If we give our word, then abandon it, people won't believe anything we say. They may doubt that God's promises are true and ridicule the notion that He is a promise keeper—all because we didn't keep our agreements.

Jesus is proof that God has kept His commitment, His pledge to us. Christ's life attests to His Father's desire to bring us back into relationship. His death affirms how far God was willing to go for us. And His resurrection confirms that those promises are eternal.

Let's avoid making promises we can't keep and be true to our word.

Read 2 Corinthians 1:20
Thank You, God, for keeping Your promises to me.

Count the Cost

I'll never know how much it cost to see my sin upon that cross.
HERE I AM TO WORSHIP by Tim Hughes

Selling goods is a way of life for many around the world. Tourists and street vendors engage in the game, each vying to get the better part of the deal. Vendors entice consumers with their must-have items. Buyers often haggle, hoping to pay less than wholesale.

Satan tried haggling with Jesus for the future of humankind. He offered riches, power, and world domination. The catch? Jesus had to abandon God's plan of salvation. But our Savior refused to haggle. He would not bargain with the enemy for our souls.

Jesus died for our sins. He paid full price, up front, for our salvation. It is a message worth sharing, regardless of what it costs us. It is a message worth living, even when it costs us more than we think we can afford.

Read Mark 15:30
Jesus, thank You for paying the ultimate price for my salvation.

The White Flag

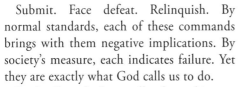

All to Jesus I surrender, all to Him I freely give.
I will ever love and trust Him, in His presence daily live.
I Surrender All by Judson W. Van deVenter

Submit. Face defeat. Relinquish. By normal standards, each of these commands brings with them negative implications. By society's measure, each indicates failure. Yet they are exactly what God calls us to do.

In the Gospels, Jesus talks about this very thing—denying one's self. He goes so far as to say, "Whoever loses their life for my sake will find it" (Matthew 10:39 NIV). It all seems to contradict what we know. Surrender seems like a setback to us. However, when we surrender to the Creator and Lord of all, when we willingly give ourselves over to His will, we gain eternity. Jesus Himself surrendered to His Father's will. Perhaps that's how He kept His eternal purpose so sharply in focus, even while facing a daily inundation of pressing need.

Excuse yourself from the struggles of this world and engage in soul surrender.

Read John 12:25
Jesus, thank You for losing Your life so I can have eternity.

Follow the Leader

And I will follow You all of my days.
Step by Step by David Strasser

Remember the children's game "Simon Says"? "Simon," the appointed leader, would instruct all the players to take action—or not, depending on whether Simon said to. Much of the fun was in seeing who could listen the longest to Simon's instructions and who would get caught off guard.

When it comes to your own life, how are you doing at following your leader, Christ? Do you consult with Him first and wait for His direction? Or do you rush ahead and then have to backtrack because you left His side? Are you struggling to let Him lead you? What are some ways in which you can pay better attention to Him?

Commit today to seeking His face first, before you call or e-mail somebody else for advice. God knows the game plan and every move to be made. Listen for His voice.

Read Psalm 63:1
Lord, I will follow You wherever you go.

Coming Home

Love divine, so great and wondrous! All my sins He then forgave.
will sing His praise forever, for His blood, His power to save.
He the Pearly Gates Will Open by Fred Blom

Unfortunately, we all know someone who has battled, or is currently battling, cancer. People we love face rounds of chemotherapy, radiation, surgery, and oncology visits. Sometimes they beat it; other times, the cancer overpowers their weakened bodies and the Lord calls them home. Yet despite cancer's mortal victory, those who are children of God achieve the ultimate triumph—eternal life with our Savior!

Our earthly choices determine where we spend eternity. Even though we may cry tears of grief at a loved one's passing, we can hold on to hope and joy—celebrating life. We can praise God that, in His compassion, He provided a Redeemer to assure our eternal home in heaven. If our lives are founded on Jesus and built on His teachings, we will someday dwell with Him forever. Even in loss, isn't it good to know that the greatest act of love—Jesus's sacrificial death—provides us a way to enter God's heavenly kingdom? Because of Jesus, we get to come Home.

Read Revelation 22:14
Thank You for the love that saves us.

My Purpose Is...

Your will above all else my purpose remains.
FROM THE INSIDE OUT by Joel Houston

For most of us, seeking our purpose in life is an exercise in trial and error. Some folks determine their mission very early on, but most of us take more time. We try different careers, spouses, and houses, but nothing seems to fill the void.

The problem is, finding your purpose has nothing to do with your degree, mate, address, or career. In fact, if you're trying to find God's purpose for your life by looking for something materialistic, you'll likely never find an answer.

The key to discovering God's purpose for your life can only be found in Him. He has special plans for your life, plans to bless you and prosper you. He promises that if you call upon Him in prayer with an open heart, He will hear you and respond.

God created each of us with a specific purpose. We only need to respond in faith and obedience when He calls.

Read Jeremiah 29:11–13
Gracious God, as I seek Your will, direct my feet.

As God Loved

O dearly, dearly has He loved, and we must love Him too,
and trust in His redeeming blood, and try His works to do.
THERE IS A GREEN HILL FAR AWAY by Cecil Frances Alexander

The depth of a mother's love is nearly impossible to capture in words, though many great writers have tried. Even for Mom, it's difficult to articulate. There's almost nothing that she won't do for her children. The level of sacrifice, compassion, and hope she has for each child seems limitless. Even when her kids fail her, a loving mother never stops caring.

Our heavenly Father loved us before we knew what love was—before we could even consider whether to return that love. Jesus modeled that divine love all the way to the cross. The least we can do is return that love by graciously serving Him and others.

Search for ways to do good works, in His name, today.

Read Hebrews 13:12
Lord, give me a servant's heart today.

Spread the News

And publish abroad His wonderful name; the name, all victorious, of Jesus extol.
Ye Servants of God by Charles Wesley

Electronic books, e-readers, websites, blogs, and social media pages are radically changing how we receive and digest information and thought. If there's something on your mind, you can "tweet" 140 characters to your family and friends. Or text to your favorite social media page, or post it to your blog. Then sit back and marvel at the responses.

As you do so, consider who might be reading what you write. At any given moment people from India, China, Africa—or those just around the corner from you—could read your words. What an opportunity to share the gospel.

Your witty online discourses may make people laugh. Your Christ-centered online messages and thoughtful postings could lead them to Christ. Consider the possibilities! Publish abroad His wonderful name.

Read Revelation 7:10
Father, help me tailor my online time to a higher purpose than fun.

Freedom from Strife

His name shall be the Counselor, the mighty Prince of Peace,
of all earth's kingdoms Conqueror, whose reign shall never cease.
BLESSED BE THE NAME by William H. Clark

It can be confusing when people call Jesus the Prince of Peace and then later refer to Him as a Mighty Warrior. Is He the one who came to bring peace on earth or the one who has crushed Satan under His feet?

The truth is, He's both. When we comprehend that there is no real peace until evil is defeated, we understand why we needed Jesus to come and save us. He brought peace to our souls by conquering the things that had ripped them apart in the first place. He flattened the torturer and set us free, then set to work gently restoring and repairing the damage. We find that the more we allow God to reclaim territory in our lives, the less turmoil we have on the inside. That isn't to say that we won't encounter stress and trauma on the outside—our alliance with the Warrior makes us a target for the enemy—but within, we can always draw near to our Prince of Peace and find rest, even in the midst of battle.

Read Hebrews 1:4

Father God, help me walk in the peace You won, regardless of what I face on the battlefield.

God Is Everything

You are my everything, and I will adore You.
Revelation Song by Jennie Riddle

What's your take on money? Is it the answer to everything? Or do you believe that more money causes more problems? Some of us agree with the latter—though we'd sure like to test it for ourselves! But it does seem, on the surface, that money could fix a lot of things.

After all, with an unlimited amount of it, doctors could conduct the research necessary to perhaps finally discover a cure for cancer. Money would allow us to feed the hungry of the world and build homes for the homeless. A monetary windfall might even save a few marriages by easing people's financial stress!

No doubt, we could do a lot of things with a lot of money. But "a lot of things" is not everything. Money can purchase a bed, but only God can give rest. Money can buy medicine, but only the Lord can heal. Money can buy a house, but only the Lord can make it a home.

Want to have a rich life? Seek the Lord instead of earthly treasures. It is only in Him that we live and move and have our being.

Read Acts 17:28
Lord, move me to value You above all things.

It's in the Blood

Your blood speaks a better word than all the empty claims I've heard upon the earth.
NOTHING BUT THE BLOOD by Matt Redman

Blood tests can confirm a person's lineage, illness, or health. Nowadays, blood is often used as evidence—the deciding factor in legal matters—because the DNA within it testifies to undeniable truth.

The same blood that coursed through Jesus's veins as a baby pumped through His heart as He walked among and healed people as an adult. Later, it soaked the wooden cross on which He hung, leaving proof of a horrible death by crucifixion. It lingered on the cloth wrapped around His buried body. And three days later, that same blood-stained cloth was part of the evidence that He rose from the dead.

Jesus shed His blood for us. His blood speaks more loudly than the empty claims of every false messiah. It testifies that there is no distance God won't go to save us. Accepting such a gift of sacrifice helps us understand unconditional love and experience unbelievable peace.

Read Matthew 26:28
Jesus, when I think of Your blood, I am humbled by Your love.

Loyal Subjects

'Tis the Lord the King of glory! At His feet we humbly fall.
Crown Him, crown Him, Lord of all!
WHO IS HE IN YONDER STALL? by Benjamin R. Hanby

One day every knee will humbly bend and the tongues of every nation will acknowledge the holy crown worn by Jesus Christ, King of glory and Lord of all. However, we shouldn't wait until eternity in order to fall at the feet of our Savior in worship and honor. Consider the words of the Lord's Prayer: "Thy Kingdom come, Thy will be done in earth, as it is in heaven" (Matthew 6:10 KJV).

Therefore, while on earth, we purposefully crown Him Lord each morning by acknowledging the blessing of another new day, a gift to us from Him. We humble ourselves before Him by treating others as we hope to be treated, regardless of their behavior. We reflect His light by gently sharing the story of His love and redemption. And we honor Him by obediently using the gifts given by the Holy Spirit.

What can you do today to glorify Jesus?

Read Revelation 7:14
Lord Jesus, You alone are worthy of our worship and our praise.

Eagerly Anticipated

Hark! the herald angels sing, "Glory to the newborn King;
peace on earth and mercy mild, God and sinners reconciled!"
Hark! the Herald Angels Sing by Charles Wesley

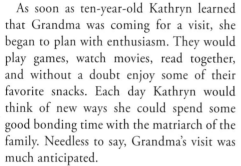

As soon as ten-year-old Kathryn learned that Grandma was coming for a visit, she began to plan with enthusiasm. They would play games, watch movies, read together, and without a doubt enjoy some of their favorite snacks. Each day Kathryn would think of new ways she could spend some good bonding time with the matriarch of the family. Needless to say, Grandma's visit was much anticipated.

Imagine how the people felt as they eagerly watched for the coming of the Messiah. Without a scheduled arrival date, they waited, all the while listening for an announcement, signs of the Promised One—hoping and hoping that the day of the Incarnation had come. His arrival finally occurred, announced with grandeur by angels appearing to humble shepherds who ran to see Him. Can you imagine it?

Have you told your neighbors that the Deliverer has come to us? Tell them today; they may still be awaiting their Savior.

Read Isaiah 7:14
Emmanuel, thank You for coming to free me from sin. Amen.

Just Leadership

He rules the world with truth and grace.

Joy to the World by Isaac Watts

Hitler. Hussein. Stalin. Lenin. Hirohito. Each one a leader overwhelmed by his hunger for world dominance. Blinded by greed and ambition, they forgot about the citizens they were supposed to lead and protect. While these are extreme examples of power in the wrong hands, we must ask ourselves, "How do I behave when given the chance to lead?" It's a tough question to answer honestly, isn't it?

Thankfully, our God is a righteous example. He rules graciously and justly. In His holiness, He has provided redemption and, therefore, the opportunity for us to know Him personally. We can praise Him because He is sovereign and merciful. All powerful. The Beginning and the End.

Praise the Lord on high, our God, who rules with truth and grace.

Read Psalm 98

I know I can trust You to lead with justice and mercy.

The Heir

No ear may hear his coming, but in this world of sin,
where meek souls will receive Him still, the dear Christ enters in.
O LITTLE TOWN OF BETHLEHEM by Phillips Brooks

The theme of hidden identity is a popular one in classic literature. Often the person with a hidden identity turns out to be the heir to a kingdom. For example, Strider in *The Lord of the Rings* is really Aragorn, the rightful king of Gondor. The boy posing as the peasant Tom Canty in most of *The Prince and the Pauper* is actually Edward Tudor, the prince of England.

Jesus, the Prince of Peace and the heir to God's kingdom, did not hide His identity, but many on earth still did not recognize Him. The people of Bethlehem did not acknowledge His coming, because He was born in powerful humility—in a stable. Even though we, like the people of Bethlehem, sometimes fail to recognize His presence, He still extends compassion toward us and stands at the door to each of our hearts, waiting for us to invite Him in.

Read Micah 5:2
Jesus, enter into my world today.

Confident Hope

Rejoice! Rejoice! Emmanuel shall come to thee, O Israel!
O Come, O Come, Emmanuel by John M. Neale

From childhood discipline and academic pressures to family and career decisions, life's challenges are constant. We see it as neighbors clamor for happiness, success, and love, only to find brief glimpses of satisfaction. Despite even the greatest triumphs, worry and pain always seem to linger somewhere in the background. The "perfect life" eludes us all.

This mode of thinking can be depressing. Thankfully, God supplies a better perspective: life here on earth is preparation for eternity. In the darkness of this world, the light of Jesus shines brightly. The hope brought by the Messiah has overcome all earthly pain and suffering.

When misery seems to surround you, remember: Christ came to give us abundant new life and will return one day with a kingdom of eternal joy. In the meantime, discovering new depths of relationship with Him now brings us a measure of the satisfaction we seek.

Emmanuel, God with us...from the beginning, to the present, and always.

Read Isaiah 7:14
I lift up Your name, Father God, for fulfilling Your promises.

Undercover Savior

This, this is Christ the King, whom shepherds guard and angels sing.
WHAT CHILD IS THIS? by William C. Dix

The New Testament Gospels tell us the sky echoed with praises as angels sang on the night of Jesus's birth. His coming had been foretold for generations, but few expected that Christ the King would come to our rescue in the form of a helpless, innocent baby. In a stable, shepherds guarded the manger where the Savior of the world lay. The One who had created the angels and could command legions had arrived in the most modest way possible to humble parents.

What Child is this? He is Immanuel—"God with us"—Messiah, the Word, King of kings, Savior, the Good Shepherd, Prince of Peace, and Lamb of God. What Child is this? His name is Jesus. The Promised One who would grow to become the man, whose faithful obedience to His heavenly Father's will would conquer sin and death's grip over the souls of all mankind.

To receive Jesus as your personal Savior, read Romans 10:9 and do as it asks; celebrate Joy coming into this world. Put your trust in Christ the King.

Read Luke 1:66
No words can express my gratitude for Your birth, precious Savior.

Super Verb

Truly He taught us to love one another; His law is love, and His gospel is peace.
O Holy Night! by John S. Dwight

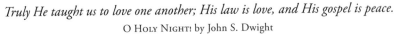

Jesus said the two greatest commandments are to love God with all our heart, soul, mind, and strength, and to love our neighbors as ourselves. Surely He meant for us to see the connection between the two. When we discover the depth of our heavenly Father's sacrificial love, we are compelled to devote ourselves to Him and to His service.

Then, as we follow in the footsteps of Christ our Savior, we are called to generously love others, just as He did. We begin to understand that the gospel is not just a noun; its core message propels us into action. His command to love requires us to give more than lip service to our beliefs; it's being His hands and feet—embodying our Savior's love in all we do and say.

Where will you share His gospel today? May others experience the love of Jesus through you.

Read Luke 1:35
Father, help me to be Your hands and feet in a world that needs You.

The Perfect Storm

When the howling storms of doubt and fear assail; by the living Word of God I shall prevail.
STANDING ON THE PROMISES by R. Kelso Carter

We've all experienced them—storms of doubt and fear. They rage up, sometimes unexpectedly, catching us unaware like waves crashing over us. Though we try to hold on, the circumstances of life can cause us to feel beaten, battered, and nearly drowned.

Disbelief and anxiety threaten to overwhelm even the hardiest soul—just as giant waves threaten the strongest ship. Add the swirling winds of personal problems and you've got a "perfect storm."

What can you do? To successfully battle the waves of doubt and fear, hoist the sail of truth that can only be found in the living Word of God. Open your Bible. Read His promises. Reflect on all the storms that God has already seen you through and trust that this storm is no different than those. Problems will come and go, but allow God to transform doubt and fear into trust and confidence.

Trust in the truth of His Word, and you will overcome.

Read Mark 4:35–41

I need to trust in Your truths, Lord. Don't let me waver.

Trusting God—Not Myself

Rid me of myself; I belong to you.

LEAD ME TO THE CROSS by Brooke Fraser

There is a story of a man who falls down into a hole. After dusting himself off, he straps his belongings to his back and begins clawing his way up the side of the hole. Halfway up, his back begins to ache and he realizes he cannot continue climbing. The weight he carries is impeding his progress, yet he hesitates. Everything he owns is in the bag and he doesn't know if he can bear leaving behind everything he holds dear. And so there he remains—burdened, stuck, and still in the hole.

We're often like that man. Even when we realize that our lives are empty, that our "stuff" is entrapping us, we're afraid to let it loose and enter God's world with nothing but the clothes on our back. Yet if we are truly born again, this is exactly what God is calling us to do. We have to let go of the mistaken belief that we can do it on our own. We have to let go of the idea that our belongings will give us security. Only then can we experience how belonging to Him gives us peace.

Read Luke 9:23
Jesus, take control of my life and lead me in the way You want me to go.

Unmerited Love

Love sent my Savior to die in my stead—why should He love me so?
Why Should He Love Me So? by Robert Harkness

Love will make you do strange things, won't it? One mother restrained herself from confronting the girl who broke her teenage son's heart. A son gave up his life so his mother and brother could be saved from floodwaters. A father sacrificed by working two jobs so his children could have a better life than he did.

For the people we love, we do the unthinkable. But none of our heroism compares to God's love for us. He deemed us so special that He took unprecedented measures to care for us, despite our selfishness and sin. Why? The simple answer is His immeasurable love. Nothing can separate us from it.

Isn't it a blessing to know there's nothing you can do to mess up or make God stop loving you? You are lovely to God. Praise Him today for the undeserved love that He holds out to you.

Read Genesis 32:10
Lord, I am speechless at the depth of Your love for me.

Hold On!

Thine forever, and should I fainting be, Lord, let me never, never outlive my love to Thee.
O SACRED HEAD, NOW WOUNDED by Bernard of Clairvaux

There comes a time in all our lives when things don't go quite as expected. Maybe you're having problems at work, your children are in trouble, your marriage is on the rocks, or you're having health problems. Having to face life's difficulties is enough to make anyone want to give up. After all, what's the point of trying to do the right thing if things continually turn out wrong?

During such times, remember the words of the apostle Paul: "Let's not get tired of doing what is good. At just the right time we will reap a harvest of blessing if we don't give up" (Galatians 6:9 NLT). Sure, it is difficult to persevere. But as the saying goes, "When you reach the end of your rope, tie a knot and hold on, help is on the way." How do you hold on? Start by praising God in the middle of your turmoil. A little praise goes a long, long way in expressing your commitment to God.

Read Galatians 6:1–10
Gracious Father, help me to persevere and trust You until I see You face-to-face.

His Will Be Done

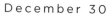

And in my heart I pray You'd let Your will be done.
'Til I See You by Joel Houston and Jadwin Gillies

A last will and testament purposefully guides families and friends in the aftermath of a person's death. It becomes the "marching orders" for every conceivable situation the deceased had the forethought to document. Done well, there's no guessing to be done about funeral arrangements, ownership of possessions, or monies left in a savings account.

When frayed nerves prevail and grief-stricken hearts cry for relief, a will can bring clarity and final authority. Of course, some people may contest it, feeling it's unfair. But the ironclad nature of wills means they can't be broken simply because two different aunts want the dishes, or because one's siblings feel they deserve the corporate stock.

God's will is ironclad, covering our temporal and eternal lives. It's specific, unchangeable—and available to sincere seekers. Knowing His will is often easier than we imagine: the Bible and the Holy Spirit reveal it. The challenge? Praying and allowing God's will to be done, regardless of how we feel about it.

Read Romans 12:2
Lord, help me to allow Your will to be done in my life.

Scatter the Darkness

He wraps Himself in light, and darkness tries to hide, and trembles at His voice.
How Great Is Our God by Chris Tomlin, Jesse Reeves, and Ed Cash

Our earth is over 93 million miles from the sun, yet the time it takes for light to travel from the sun to our atmosphere is less than nine minutes. While scientists have measured the speed of light, it is impossible for the human eye to see light move, or for our minds to fully comprehend its speed.

God is light. The Bible tells us that there is no darkness in Him at all, and that darkness can't even comprehend Him. If we consider this fact, then we must come to the conclusion that God can and does act with mind-bending speed. He hears our prayers the moment we speak them. He goes before us, lighting the way on the path He provided.

Darkness may try to hide, but it can't move fast enough to avoid the light! It only has time to tremble before it is utterly scattered by the light of God's glory.

Allow God to wrap you in His light and scatter your darkness today.

Read 1 John 1:5
God, bring Your light into my darkened world today.